The Essence of Herbal and Floral Teas

Also by Mary El-Baz

Flavoring with Culinary Herbs: Tips, Recipes, and Cultivation

Easy and Healthful Mediterranean Cooking

Building a Healthy Lifestyle: A Simple Nutrition and Fitness Approach

The Essence of Herbal and Floral Teas

Mary El-Baz, Ph.D.

iUniverse, Inc.
New York Lincoln Shanghai

The Essence of Herbal and Floral Teas

Copyright © 2006 by Mary El-Baz

All rights reserved. No part of this book may be used or reproduced by any means, graphic, electronic, or mechanical, including photocopying, recording, taping or by any information storage retrieval system without the written permission of the publisher except in the case of brief quotations embodied in critical articles and reviews.

iUniverse books may be ordered through booksellers or by contacting:

iUniverse
2021 Pine Lake Road, Suite 100
Lincoln, NE 68512
www.iuniverse.com
1-800-Authors (1-800-288-4677)

The information, ideas and suggestions in this book are not intended as a substitute for professional medical advice. Before following any suggestions contained in this book, you should first consult your personal physician.
Neither the author nor the publisher shall be liable or responsible for any loss or damage allegedly arising as a consequence of your use or application of any information or suggestions in this book.

ISBN-13: 978-0-595-41026-2 (pbk)
ISBN-13: 978-0-595-85380-9 (ebk)
ISBN-10: 0-595-41026-X (pbk)
ISBN-10: 0-595-85380-3 (ebk)

Printed in the United States of America

—To my family and friends who take pleasure in the soothing and invigorating essences of herbs and flowers

Contents

Herbal and Floral Teas, Infusions, or Tisanes? 1
Herbs and Edible Flowers 6
    Calendula 6
        Calendula Herb Tisane Blend 6
        Orange Spice Calendula Floral Tea Blend 7
    Catnip 7
        Catnip Tisane 7
        Smoothing Evening Tisane 8
        Peppy Catnip Blend 8
    Chamomile 9
        Chamomile Cooler 9
        Tangy Chamomile Cranberry Tisane 10
    Hibiscus 10
        Fancy Hibiscus Tea 11
        Hibiscus Sun Tisane 11
        Caribbean Hibiscus Cooler 12
    Honeysuckle 12
        Honeysuckle Tisane 12
        Honeysuckle Black Rice Pudding with Coconut Cream 13
    Jasmine 14
        Jasmine Lemonade 15
        White Grape and Jasmine Cooler 15
        Hot Jasmine Tea 16
    Lavender 16
        French Garden Iced Tea 16

    Lavender Rosemary Mint Tisane 17
Lemon Balm 17
    Golden Lemon Balm Tisane 18
    Spring Herbal Tisane. 18
Lemon Verbena 19
    Lemon Verbena Syrup. 19
    Rose Hip Lemon Tisane 20
Mint—Spearmint and Peppermint 20
    Moroccan Mint Tea. 21
    Peppermint Tisane. 21
Pink (Dianthus) 22
    Clove-scented Pink Jelly. 22
    Tea Sandwich Spread. 24
Rose. 24
    Easy Rose Hip Tea. 24
    Drying Rose Hips 25
    Rose Water 25
Rosemary. 26
    Rosemary Tisane 27
    Lemon-Rosemary Sparkling Tea 27
Scented Geranium 28
    Orange-scented Geranium Iced Tea. 28
    Ginger-scented Geranium Honey 29
Sweet Violet. 30
    Violet Leaf Tisane 30
    Violet Lassi 31

Sweeteners 32
    Flower Sugar 32
    Flower Syrup 32
    Flower Honey 32

Lemonades and Spritzers 34
    Jasmine Limeade 34
    Chamomile Pear Cider 34

Chamomile Apple Cider..35
　　Lavender White Wine Spritzer................................35
　　Diabolo Violette Spritzer.....................................36
　　Jasmine Vodka Spritzer.......................................36
　　Flower Basket Tea..37
　　Chamomile Iced Tisane Spritzer..............................38

Ices and Frozen Treats...40
　　Herbal and Floral Ice Cubes..................................40
　　Strawberry-Rose Petal Ice....................................40
　　Easy Lemon-Peppermint Ice...................................41
　　Pineapple-Mint Freeze.......................................42
　　Raspberry-Hibiscus Sorbet...................................42
　　Ultimate Hibiscus Slush......................................43
　　Violet Lavender Sorbet......................................43
　　Gillyflower Sorbet...44
　　Violet Milkshake...45

Sangrias, Party Punches, and Spirits.............................46
　　Lemon Balm Sangria..46
　　Lavender Chardonnay Sangria.................................46
　　Mulled Rosemary Tea Wine....................................47
　　Rose-scented Geranium Strawberry Punch......................47
　　Fruity Mint Punch..48
　　Hibiscus Grape Champagne Punch..............................49
　　Lavender Martini...49
　　Etincelle de Nuit...50
　　Rose-scented Geranium Raspberry Liqueur.....................51
　　Rose Cordial...51

Herbal and Floral Tisane Blends.................................53
　　Tea Party Tisane Blend.......................................53
　　Lemon Mint Cooler...53
　　Soothing Essence Tisane Blend................................53
　　Chamomile Rose Herbal Blend.................................54

    Pink Rose Tisane Blend 54
    Nitey-Nite Tisane Blend 54
    Chamomile Apple Tisane Blend 55
    Orange Spice Tisane Blend 55

Flavored Tea Blends 56
    Southern Mint Tea Blend 56
    Night Jasmine Tea Blend 56
    Zingy Tea Blend 56
    Apple Spice Tea Blend 57
    Floral Sachet Tea Blend 57
    Lavender Green Tea Blend 57
    White-Pink-Rose Geranium Tea Blend 58

Confections 59
    Raspberry and Violet Tarlets 59
    Candied Violets 60
    Floral Sprinkles Angel Food Cake 61
    Dried Edible Flower Sprinkles 62
    Candied Rose Hips 63

Cultivating Culinary Herbs and Edible Flowers 64
    In the Garden 65
    Indoors 65
    Propagation 66
    Diseases and Insect Pests 67
    Harvesting and Preserving 68
        Drying Herbs and Flowers 69
        Freezing Herbs and Flowers 69

Culture Information for Culinary Herbs and Edible Flowers 71
    Calendula (*Calendula officinalis*) 71
    Catnip (*Nepeta cataria*) 71
    Chamomile, Roman (*Chamaemelum nobile*) 72
    Chamomile, German (*Matricaria recutita*) 72
    Hibiscus (*Hibiscus sabdariffa*) 73

Honeysuckle (*Lonicera japonica*) 73
Jasmine (*Jasminum sambac*) 74
Lavender (*Lavandula angustifolia*) 74
Lemon Balm (*Melissa officinalis*) 75
Lemon Verbena (*Aloysia triphylla*) 75
Mint (*Mentha* species and cultivars) 76
Pink (*Dianthus* species and cultivars) 76
Rose (*Rosa* species and cultivars) 77
Rosemary (*Rosmarinus officinalis*) 77
Scented Geranium (*Pelargonium* species) 78
Sweet Violet (*Viola odorata*) 79

About the Author 81
Index 83

Herbal and Floral Teas, Infusions, or Tisanes?

Herbs and flowers have long been used for their medicinal and soothing properties throughout history, whether by eating, applying topically, or by drinking. Culinary herbs are ones which fresh or dried leaves are used in cooking. Some of the common culinary herbs are basil, tarragon, rosemary, mint, and thyme. Flower cuisine has been traced back to Roman times, and to the Chinese, Middle Eastern, and Indian cultures. Flower or floral waters are used primarily in the cuisines of India, the Middle East, and Eastern Europe. Throughout Turkey, Lebanon, Syria, Egypt, Tunisia, and Morocco, pastries, puddings and other sweets are scented with either rose or orange-blossom water. Edible flowers were especially popular in the Victorian era during Queen Victoria's reign. Flower waters were very popular for flavoring cakes or for adding delicate flavors to jams and jellies. Today we use them in teas or as a garnish for desserts. Many restaurant chefs and home cooks garnish their entrees with flower blossoms for a touch of elegance. The secret to success when using edible flowers and flower waters is to use them sparingly. Flower waters can add a delightful, mysterious, subtle flavor to beverages and sweets.

Many of the herbs and flowers used in beverages are known for their stimulating or relaxing effect much the same as tea or coffee. The phrase "herbal teas" has become a generic term for herbs, edible flowers, and spices steeped in hot water whether or not actual tea leaves are used. If tea leaves are not used, these beverages are known as herbal infusions or "tisanes," served either warm or cold as medicinal home remedies or simply as pleasant and relaxing drinks. Tisane was originally a French word for an herbal infusion that had beneficial or healthful properties

Herbal tisanes contain none of the tannin or caffeine found in most teas. Tisanes are made of herbs, flowers, leaves and fruit pieces, singly or as a blend from a mixture of various herbs. Advocates of homeopathic remedies regularly recommend tisanes for their healing properties, whether to heal, cure, prevent illnesses and diseases, to lose weight, purify the blood, or cleanse the body.

Popular culinary herbs and edible flowers are often used for tisanes. Mint helps with digestion and has so many different varieties that it mixes well with many herbs. Spearmint and peppermint tisanes are often used as revitalizing drinks and can be especially refreshing served ice cold on a hot summer day. Lemon balm has been known to calm the nerves and aid in digestion also. Chamomile is said to calm nerves and aid in sleep as well as being good for the digestive system. Lavender calms the nerves and continues to be a popular remedy for sore throats and head colds. A tisane of violets and rose petals sweetened with honey can soothe a cough. Hibiscus and rose hips, which are rich in vitamin C, can produce a rich fruity tisane with a beautiful red color.

Tisanes can either be drunk in the morning instead of coffee or tea to invigorate, or in the evening to soothe and relax. Some herbs and flowers that produce invigorating teas include peppermint, spearmint, rose hips, roses, and hibiscus blossoms. Herbs with a sedative or relaxing effect include lavender, sweet violet flowers and leaves, and chamomile.

This book presents herbal and floral tea recipes that you can prepare at home. The herbs and edible flowers used in the recipes can be purchased from herbal and natural product stores or can be cultivated in your own herbal and flower gardens. Here's a simple list of herbs and edible flowers to purchase or cultivate to help you determine which method you want to use.

Herbs and Flowers to Purchase

- Calendula
- Catnip
- Chamomile
- Hibiscus blossoms
- Honeysuckle
- Jasmine
- Lavender
- Lemon balm
- Lemon verbena

- Pink (Dianthus)
- Peppermint and spearmint
- Rose petals and rose hips
- Rosemary
- Scented-leaf geranium
- Sweet violet

Herbs and Flowers to Cultivate

- Calendula
- Catnip
- Chamomile
- Lavender
- Lemon balm
- Lemon verbena
- Pink (Dianthus)
- Peppermint and spearmint
- Roses and rose hips
- Rosemary
- Scented-leaf geranium
- Sweet violet

Preparing tisanes with herbs and edible flowers is easy. Fresh or dried herbs and flowers may be used. Dried herbs and flowers can easily be substituted for fresh ones at the ratio of one (dried) to three (fresh); that is, for one teaspoon of dried herb leaves or flower petals, use one tablespoon of fresh leaves or petals. When using edible flowers, pinch off the white part at the base of petals, as this is bitter.

A cautionary note on flowers: Not all flowers are edible; some may taste bad and some are poisonous. Eat only flowers that you are certain are edible. A flower is not necessarily edible because it is served with food. The edible flowers presented in this book are considered edible; however you may wish to consult a good reference book to find other edible flowers. Do not eat flowers from florists, nurseries, garden centers, or flowers found on the side of the road. Eat only flowers that you or someone else have grown specifically for culinary purposes. If you have hay fever, asthma, or allergies, it may be wise not to eat flowers since many allergies are due to sensitivity to pollen of specific plants. And as with introducing any new food into your diet, introduce flowers into your diet one at a time and in small quantities.

Here are the basic directions for making a pot of hot herbal or iced herbal tisane, or tisanes made with spices, crushed seeds, and roots.

Basic Directions for Preparing a Tisane

1. Measure one level teaspoon of dried herb leaves or petals to a cup of boiling water. If fresh herbs are used, measure one level tablespoonful per cup.

2. Steep the infusion for five to ten minutes, then strain leaves, serve, and enjoy. Sweeten with honey or sugar to taste, and, if desired, serve with a slice of lemon.

Basic Iced Herbal Tisane

Brew the same as for hot tea but after straining the herbs from the liquid, cool to room temperature then pour over ice.

For Tisanes Made with Spices, Crushed Seeds and Roots

1. In a saucepan, bring water to a boil.

2. Add the spices, seeds, or roots directly to the boiling water, let it simmer for five minutes, and then let it steep, covered, for an additional five minutes.

3. Strain both herbal and root tisanes after steeping.

Keep in mind that herbs and flowers are not just for tisanes and teas! There's so much more: lemonades, spritzers, sangrias, ices, sorbets, sweeteners, and sweet treats. Get the sublime flavor and fragrances of flowers with flower sugars, syrups, and honeys. They bring a fascinating aspect to iced or hot teas, lemonades, and desserts. Flower syrups are delicious on pancakes and waffles. Butter whipped with flower honey is scrumptious on just-from-the-oven breads and muffins. Some of the best herbs and flowers to use in flavoring sugars, syrups, and honeys are the flowers of clove-scented pink, lavender, scented geranium, sweet violet, rose, jasmine, and honeysuckle.

This little recipe and idea guide will acquaint you with a few of the common culinary herbs and edible flowers used in brewing refreshing and stimulating or calming beverages or delectable desserts, as well as tips for growing these herbs and edible flowers so they are available to you practically year-round. There is a selection of recipes featuring sweeteners, lemonades and spritzers, ices and frozen treats, sangrias, party punches, spirits, herbal and floral tisane blends, flavored tea blends, and confections. Following the recipes are cultivation and preservation basics for the herbs and edible flowers used in the recipes that you may wish to grow to use in your cooking.

Herbs and Edible Flowers

CALENDULA

Calendula (*Calendula officinalis*), or pot marigold, is grown in gardens around the world, but is native to the Mediterranean countries. Calendula has pretty petals in golden-orange hues and its flavor ranges from spicy to bitter, tangy to peppery. Their sharp taste resembles saffron which causes it to be also known as "poor man's saffron." The name, calendula, refers to the plant's tendency to bloom in accordance with the calendar—every month in some regions, or during the new moon. In the sixteenth century, marigold was a common garden plant valued by herbalists for comforting the heart and soothing the spirit. The dried flowers went into the making of broths and teas, and were used to add color to cheese. The Egyptians valued the marigold as a rejuvenating herb, and the Greeks garnished and flavored food with its golden petals.

The flowers contain high concentrations of colorful orange xanthophylls, carotenoids and other flavonoids that are powerful antioxidants. Calendula has a distinguished healing reputation and was used in Indian, Arabic, and Greek traditional medicine. It is said that such large amounts of it are grown in Russia for medicinal uses that it is called "the Russian penicillin." Calendula flower preparations were observed to be anti-inflammatory and astringent. In both contemporary and historic times, calendula tinctures, ointments, and washes have been used to notably speed the healing of burns, bruises, cuts, and the minor infections that they cause.

Be sure that the marigold that you purchase or grow says *Calendula officinalis*. Calendula officinalis is sometimes confused with *Tagetes* species of marigolds, more frequently planted in gardens than calendula.

Calendula Herb Tisane Blend

¼ cup dried applemint leaves
2 tablespoons dried rosemary

2 tablespoons dried lemon balm leaves
1 tablespoon dried calendula petals
3 tablespoons dried chamomile flowers

Combine the dried herbs together and store in an airtight container. To make tea, use one heaping teaspoon of blend per cup of water.

Makes ¾ cup

Orange Spice Calendula Floral Tea Blend

2 cups dried orange-scented geranium leaves
¼ cup loose black tea leaves leaves
1 teaspoon ground cloves
1 cup dried calendula petals
1 tablespoon dried orange peel
1 tablespoon dried lemon peel

Combine the dried herbs together and store in an airtight container. To make tea, use one heaping teaspoon of blend per cup of water.

Makes about 3½ cups

CATNIP

Catnip (*Nepeta cataria*) has many medicinal and culinary uses. Catnip makes a tasty and healthful herb tea. Catnip has tonic, stimulant, nervine, and antispasmodic properties. Catnip has been used historically as a soothing nighttime tea to settle children into sleep. As a gentle before meal tea, catnip acts to stimulate the digestive system and increase appetites.

If you choose to grow catnip in your garden, guard it from cats! Those furry felines can tear the little plants to pieces!

Catnip Tisane

1 teaspoon dried catnip leaves
1 cup boiling water

1 lemon slice

1. Place leaves in a small teapot.
2. Pour boiling water over leaves.
3. Steep for 5 minutes.
4. Strain and pour into a cup. Add the juice of one lemon slice.

Serves 1

Smoothing Evening Tisane

Perfect for young children!

½ teaspoon dried catnip leaves
½ teaspoon dried chamomile flowers
1 cup boiling water

1. Place leaves in a small teapot.
2. Pour boiling water over leaves.
3. Steep for 5 to 10 minutes.
4. Strain and pour into a cup.

Serves 1

Peppy Catnip Blend

½ teaspoon dried catnip leaves
½ teaspoon dried peppermint leaves
1 cup boiling water

1. Place leaves in a small teapot.
2. Pour boiling water over leaves.
3. Steep for 5 to 10 minutes.

4. Strain and pour into a cup.

Serves 1

CHAMOMILE

Chamomile bears small, daisy-like flowers that have long been used in Europe for tea. Chamomile has a soft, subtle, sweet apple-like flavor. German chamomile (*Matricaria recutita*) is a two-foot annual and Roman chamomile (*Chamaemelum nobile*) is a lush green perennial plant that bears small, yellow, button-like flowers. Many references designate German chamomile as the sweeter type preferred for tea. However, both chamomiles are perfect for a light, apple-scented tea.

Chamomile is well known for a variety of medicinal properties. It has been used throughout history for its calmative effects. Roman chamomile is brewed into a tea and served as a soothing tonic which helps those who suffer from insomnia. It also stimulates a wane appetite and improves digestion.

A few of the uses for this herb include tea, as a garnish for decorating foods with the edible flowers on the stems, as a herbal medication for use in relieving stomach discomfort, some skin irritations, as a flavoring or coloring agent used in various beverages such as vermouth or making wine, and as an ingredient used in making cosmetics. People who are sensitive to daisies may indicate that this herb will also cause an allergic reaction, so it is best to know if one is sensitive to chamomile before using it for any purpose.

Chamomile Cooler

6 cups water
½ cup dried chamomile flowers
2 tablespoons dried lemon verbena leaves
⅓ cup honey
Ice cubes

1. Warm a teapot.

2. In a tea kettle, bring the 6 cups of water to a boil.

3. Place flowers and herb leaves into the teapot. Pour boiling water into the teapot.

4. Cover and steep for 10 minutes.

5. Stir in honey and allow to dissolve.

6. Fill four tall glasses with ice, pour tea over ice through a strainer, and serve immediately.

Serves 6

Tangy Chamomile Cranberry Tisane

4 chamomile teabags
4 cups water
1 cup cranberry juice cocktail, at room temperature
Sugar to taste

1. Warm a teapot.

2. In a tea kettle, bring the 4 cups of water to a boil.

3. Place teabags into the teapot. Pour boiling water into the teapot.

4. Cover and steep for 10 minutes.

5. Stir in cranberry juice.

6. Pour tea into cups, add sugar to taste, and serve.

Serves 4

HIBISCUS

Red hibiscus blossoms (*Hibiscus sadariffa*) have a cranberry-like flavor with citrus overtones and are high in vitamin C. Hibiscus is an ingredient in red zinger tea, mixed with any number of other herbs. Its slightly acidic flower petals are a good addition to spicy salads, and it makes a fruity, fragrant smoke for meats and fish.

The tart, bright red hibiscus tea is known in Arabic as "karkady," and is very popular in Africa, especially in Egypt and the Sudan. During the Islamic fasting month of Ramadan, many Egyptian families will break their day-long fast at sunset with glasses of karkady instead of a traditional apricot drink. Beverages made of hibiscus are also popular in Central America and the Caribbean, as well as the use of the fleshy calyxes (fresh or dried) in making roselle wine, tea, jelly, syrup, marmalade, ices, ice cream, sherbets, butter, pudding, pies and cakes, tarts, gelatin, and to color and flavor rum.

Fancy Hibiscus Tea

6 cups water
3 cinnamon sticks, broken up
1 tablespoon loose black, green, or roobis tea leaves
2 tablespoons dried hibiscus flowers, crumbled
1½ tablespoons honey, to taste
Fresh mint leaves or orange slices, for garnish

1. In a large saucepan, bring water to a light simmer, then turn off heat, and add the cinnamon sticks, tea, and hibiscus flowers.

2. Cover and allow to steep for 15 to 20 minutes. If a stronger flavor is desired, use more herbs, because longer steeping may bring out a bitter flavor.

3. Strain liquid mixture into a pitcher, then add the honey to taste.

4. Serve over ice (if desired), and garnish with fresh mint and/or slices of oranges.

Serves 6

Hibiscus Sun Tisane

4 cups water
2 tablespoons dried hibiscus flowers, crumbled

1. In a large glass jar, soak the dried hibiscus flowers in cold water for two days.

2. Strain and serve over ice.

Serves 4

Caribbean Hibiscus Cooler

4 cups cold water
½ cup dried hibiscus flowers, crumbled
⅓ cup sugar
2 cups ice
Orange slices

1. In a large saucepan, bring water to a light simmer.

2. Add the hibiscus flowers and simmer over moderate heat for 5 minutes. Remove saucepan from heat.

3. Cover and allow to steep for 30 minutes.

4. Strain, pressing flowers to express liquid,

5. Pour into a pitcher, add sugar and ice, stirring until sugar is dissolved.

6. Chill cooler and stir before serving. Garnish with orange slices.

Serves 6

HONEYSUCKLE

Japanese Honeysuckle (*Lonicera japonica*) is best known for its sweet-smelling flowers. They are white at first, turning yellow as they get older. It is an herb used primarily in Traditional Chinese Medicine (TCM). It is found in many cleansing and detoxifying blends because of its ability to clear heat, wind, and toxins from the blood and liver. It is commonly used for sore throat, fever, skin blemishes, and rashes because of its anti-inflammatory, fever-reducing, and antimicrobial properties.

Honeysuckle is popular in Asian cuisine, especially in desserts. Honeysuckle combines well with chrysanthemum flowers for a wonderful beverage.

Honeysuckle leaves contain toxic saponins, so use only the flowers.

Honeysuckle Tisane

½ cup dried honeysuckle flowers

½ cup dried chrysanthemum flowers
4 cups water

1. Warm a teapot.

2. In a tea kettle, bring the 4 cups of water to a boil.

3. Place flowers into the teapot. Pour boiling water into the teapot.

4. Cover and steep for 10 minutes.

5. Strain tea into cups and serve.

Serves 4

Honeysuckle Black Rice Pudding with Coconut Cream

½ cup Thai black glutinous rice
½ cup dried honeysuckle flowers
1¾ cups boiling water
1½ to 2 tablespoons sugar
1 cup frozen thick coconut milk, thawed
4 teaspoons fine rice flour
¼ teaspoon kosher salt

Pre-soak rice and flowers:

1. Soak rice in warm water to cover by at least 1 inch for from 2 hours to overnight.

2. Float honeysuckle flowers in ½ cup warm water, cover, and let steep at room temperature overnight.

Prepare a steamer, using a 14-inch wok, a Dutch oven, or stockpot:

1. Place a steaming rack in pot and pour in at least 2 inches of water (rack should be above water level). Cover and bring to a boil.

2. Drain rice and place in a wide, shallow bowl. Place bowl on rack in steamer. Add the 1¾ cups boiling water to rice, cover steamer and cook for 1 to 1½ hours, adding more boiling water to steamer as needed to keep the water level fairly constant.

3. The rice is done when it is soft, and liquid almost soaked up and a little creamy. The rice will be a bit crunchy on the outside, but creamy in the center.

4. Remove the honeysuckle flowers from the flower water. Warm soaking water a little, then stir in sugar until just dissolved, adjusting sweetness as desired. Be careful heating the water, if it gets too hot, it will lose its aroma. Pour scented water over rice and stir gently. Refrigerate if not serving immediately.

Prepare coconut cream:

1. Pour the coconut milk into a small saucepan and place over medium-high heat, whisk in rice flour and cook until just thickened. Stir in salt.

To serve: If rice has been refrigerated, reheat it in a steamer, or microwave until warm. Spoon rice into bowls and top with 3 to 4 tablespoons of the thickened coconut milk.

Serves 4

Jasmine

Jasmine flowers (*Jasminum sambac*) are intensely fragrant and are traditionally used for scenting tea. Jasmine is known in India as the "Queen of the Night" because of its intoxicating perfume that is released at night. In Ayurvedic medicine, jasmine is used to calm the nerves and sooth emotional problems. In Chinese medicine, jasmine flowers are known to "cool" the blood, revitalize, and restore the balance of energy, and have strong antibacterial and antiviral properties.

Jasmine is used in teas, sweet confections, herbal baths, skin creams, soaps and potpourri. It is also used as a decorative touch to special dishes.

Jasmine Lemonade

4 cups water
2 teaspoons dried jasmine flowers
Prepared chilled lemonade
Ice

1. Warm a teapot.

2. In a tea kettle, bring the 4 cups of water to a boil.

3. Place jasmine flowers in the teapot. Pour boiling water into the teapot.

4. Cover and steep for 5 minutes.

5. Fill four tall glasses with ice. Fill the glasses one-half full with tea poured through a strainer and top off with the lemonade.

6. Serve immediately.

Serves 4

White Grape and Jasmine Cooler

4 cups water
2 teaspoons dried jasmine flowers
Chilled white grape juice
Ice

1. Warm a teapot.

2. In a tea kettle, bring the 4 cups of water to a boil.

3. Place jasmine flowers in the teapot. Pour boiling water into the teapot.

4. Cover and steep for 5 minutes.

5. Fill four tall glasses with ice. Fill the glasses one-half full with tea poured through a strainer and top off with the white grape juice.

6. Serve immediately.

Serves 4

Hot Jasmine Tea

4 cups water
1 teaspoon dried jasmine flowers
2 teaspoons loose Darjeeling tea leaves
Sugar or honey, to taste

1. Warm a teapot.

2. In a tea kettle, bring the 4 cups of water to a boil.

3. Place flowers and tea into the teapot. Pour boiling water into the teapot.

4. Cover and steep for 5 to 8 minutes.

5. Pour tea into cups, add sugar or honey to taste, and serve.

Serves 4

LAVENDER

The fresh fragrance of lavender (*Lavandula angustifolia*) can be quite heady, bringing to mind soft and peaceful images. It is a plant valued throughout history for its cleansing and cosmetic properties. Lavender has a sweet, floral flavor, with lemon and citrus notes. A rule of thumb when cooking with lavender is that the darker the color of the blossom, the more intense the flavor. Use a light touch at first to test the intensity and depth of flavor, and then add more as needed. Lavender flowers look beautiful and taste delightful in a glass of champagne, with chocolate cake, or as a garnish for sorbets or ice creams. Lavender lends itself to savory dishes also, from hearty stews to wine-reduced sauces and to delicate dishes such as tea, pastry, custards, flans, or sorbets.

French Garden Iced Tea

4 cups water
1 teaspoon dried lavender flowers
3 teaspoons loose black tea leaves

Sugar or honey, to taste

1. Warm a teapot.

2. In a tea kettle, bring the 4 cups of water to a boil.

3. Place flowers and tea into the teapot. Pour boiling water into the teapot.

4. Cover and steep for 5 to 8 minutes.

5. Pour tea into cups, add sugar or honey to taste, and serve.

Serves 4

Lavender Rosemary Mint Tisane

1 teaspoon fresh lavender flowers or ½ teaspoon dried lavender flowers
1½ tablespoons fresh mint leaves or 1 teaspoon dried mint leaves
1 teaspoon dried rosemary
1 cup boiling water

1. Place leaves in a small teapot.

2. Pour boiling water over leaves.

3. Steep for 5 to 10 minutes.

4. Pour into a cup.

Serves 1

LEMON BALM

Lemon balm (*Melissa officinalis*) has a pleasing lemon flavor and fragrance that makes an enjoyable tea. The fragrance of the plant is citrusy and fresh. If the leaves are barely brushed, the scent is released. The ancient Greeks recognized this plant for both its soothing smell and its medicinal properties. Like most herbs, lemon balm is antibacterial and antiviral in nature. Londoners of Elizabethan times would carry small bouquets, called "tussie mussies," filled with aromatic herbs and flowers, including lemon balm, which they would frequently sniff to disguise unpleasant smells of the day.

Honey and lemon balm have a natural connection; the "Melissa" in lemon balm's scientific name is a Latin derivation of the Greek word for honey bee. Honey saturated with lemon balm essence has a citrus punch with a hint of mint. The taste of the leaves adds the perfect tangy note to fruit salads. Lemon balm combined with other garden herbs creates delightful herbal teas and homemade herb vinegars. For a wonderful garnish, freeze some small leaves into ice cubes to serve in lemonade.

Golden Lemon Balm Tisane

6 cups water
1 cup fresh lemon balm leaves
3 slices of lemon rind
1 tablespoon honey

1. Warm a teapot.

2. In a tea kettle, bring the 6 cups of water to a boil.

3. Place the herb leaves, lemon slices, and honey into the teapot. Pour boiling water into the teapot.

4. Cover and steep for 15 minutes.

5. Strain into cups and serve immediately.

Serves 6

Spring Herbal Tisane

6 cups water
16 fresh lemon balm leaves
12 small mint leaves
½ teaspoon dried rose petals
2 fresh rose-scented geranium leaves

1. Warm a teapot.

2. In a tea kettle, bring the 6 cups of water to a boil.

3. Place the herb and flower into the teapot. Pour boiling water into the teapot.

4. Cover and steep for 15 minutes.

5. Strain into cups and serve immediately.

Serves 6

LEMON VERBENA

The leaves and flowering tops of lemon verbena (*Aloysia triphylla*) are used in teas and to flavor alcoholic beverages. The plant is also an ingredient in some desserts, fruit salads, and jams. It is used in perfumery, especially in making toilet water and eau de cologne. Lemon verbena has a strong affinity to fresh fruits in that the subtle lemon flavor nicely emphasizes and reinforces the fruit's natural aroma. Thus, lemon verbena can be used to give fruit salads an unusual touch, chopped leaves can be sprinkled over a fruit bowl, freshly prepared fruit juice can be garnished with one or two leaves of lemon verbena, or used as a flavoring in or on fruit sorbet or ice cream.

As a medicinal plant, the leaves and flowers of lemon verbena have been used as a muscle relaxant, fever reducer, sedative, and digestive aid.

Lemon Verbena Syrup

Delicious with ice cream, pound cake, or other light desserts!

1 cup fresh lemon verbena leaves
½ cup sugar
½ cup water

1. Blanch the lemon verbena leaves in boiling water briefly to brighten the color, then immediately plunge into ice water to stop cooking.

2. In a small saucepan, combine the sugar and water, bring to a simmer, then remove from the heat and cool.

3. Place the lemon verbena and cooled syrup in a blender and purée on high for 2 minutes.

4. Chill overnight, then strain through a fine mesh strainer. Pour into a small bottle and store in the refrigerator.

Makes ½ cup

Rose Hip Lemon Tisane

4 cups water
¼ cup rose hips
½ cup torn fresh lemon verbena leaves
Honey

1. Warm a teapot.

2. In a tea kettle, bring the 4 cups of water to a boil.

3. Place the rosehips and lemon verbena into the teapot. Pour boiling water into the teapot.

4. Cover and steep for 15 minutes.

5. Strain into cups, sweeten with honey, and serve immediately.

Serves 4

Mint—Spearmint and Peppermint

There are several species and varieties of mint, such as curly-leaf mint, apple mint, and orange mint; but the common spearmint (*Mentha spicata*) and the peppermint (*M. piperita*) supply the herb and aromatic oils in general use as flavoring agents. All mints are used medicinally and in cooking. Mint has a strong, sweet flavor with a cool aftertaste. Spearmint is the one used principally in flavoring iced tea and other beverages, while peppermint is more commonly used in medicines and confections. Mint flavors drinks, candy, toothpaste, and medicine. Mint aids digestion and stomach complaints. Peppermint, in particular, has additional antiseptic and antiviral properties.

The leaves of the various species and varieties impart their pleasing flavors to tea, beverages, jellies, ice creams, confections, pea, cream of pea soup, and lamb dishes. Mint is predominant in Afghanistani, Egyptian, Indian, and Middle Eastern cuisines and in spice blends.

Moroccan Mint Tea

4 cups water
3 to 4 teaspoons loose black tea leaves or 3 to 4 tea bags
10 sprigs fresh spearmint
3 tablespoon sugar
4 sprigs of spearmint for garnish

1. Boil the water in a teakettle. Warm a 4-cup teapot.

2. Combine the tea, mint, and sugar in the teapot and add the boiling water. Leave it to brew for 2 or 3 minutes.

3. While brewing, warm glass tumblers (demitasse or a shot glass size) by rinsing in hot water. Put one sprig of mint into each tumbler. Pour tea into each tumbler through a strainer.

Serves 6

Peppermint Tisane

1 to 2 teaspoons dried peppermint leaves
1 cup boiling water

1. Place leaves in a small teapot.

2. Pour boiling water over leaves.

3. Steep for 5 to 10 minutes.

4. Pour into a cup.

Serves 1

Note: Peppermint tisane has muscle relaxant properties and therefore may relax the lower esophageal sphincter, allowing the contents of the stomach to move upwards into the esophagus. It may be wise to avoid peppermint if you have gastroesophageal reflux disease (GERD).

PINK (DIANTHUS)

Pink, also known as dianthus or carnation (*Dianthus caryophyllus*), is the miniature member of the carnation family with a light spicy, peppery clove-like or nutmeg scent. Pink used to be known as clove gillyflowers. Pinks are attractive to look at and are wonderfully fragrant. They are good candied in marmalade or as cake decorations, steeped in wine, pickled with mace and cinnamon in vinegar, or minced in stuffings, and the petals add color to salads or aspics. Carnation petals are one of secret ingredients that have been used to make Chartreuse, a French liqueur, since the seventeenth century.

Clove-scented Pink Jelly

A delightful raspberry-colored jelly!

1 to 2 cups of fresh clove-scented pink (dianthus) flowers
1½ cups boiling water
½ cup vinegar
3½ cups sugar
3 ounces liquid pectin
2 to 3 jelly jars (half-pint) for canning

Sterilize jelly jars:

1. Wash and dry jars.

2. Fill a large, deep cooking pot, half full of water. Bring to a rolling boil.

3. Place jars into the cooking pot and leave in the boiling water for 10 minutes.

4. Remove the jars from the boiling water.

Prepare jelly:

1. In a small bowl, place the clove-scented pinks and pour boiling water over them.
2. Cover and let steep for 30 minutes. Strain and measure the liquid, adding water, if necessary, to make 1½ cups.
3. In a large saucepan, add the herbal liquid, vinegar, and sugar.
4. Cook over high heat, stirring, until the mixture come to a full rolling boil.
5. Stir in 3 ounces of liquid pectin. Continue cooking and stirring until the mixture returns to a full rolling boil that can not be stirred down.
6. Cook for 1 minute more, stirring constantly.
7. Remove from heat and skim off any foam from the surface.
8. Ladle into hot, sterilized half-pint jelly jars, leaving ¼-inch headspace. Wipe the rims and attach canning lids.
9. Follow the standard directions for the boiling-water method of preserving, boiling the jars for five minutes.

Boiling water method of preserving:

1. Fill a large, deep cooking pot, half full of water. Bring to a rolling boil.
2. Place filled, lidded canning jars into the cooking pot, leaving at least 1 inch between jars.
3. Add more boiling water to the cooking pot, covering the lids by 2 inches. Cover the pot, bring to a hard boil, and boil for 5 minutes.
4. Remove the jars from the boiling water. Cool, remove bands, label, and store in a cool, dark place.

Makes 2 to 3 half-pint jars of jelly

Tea Sandwich Spread

½ cup fresh clove-scented pink (dianthus) flower petals
4 ounces cream cheese, softened

1. In a small bowl, combine the flower petals and cream cheese. Whip together until well-blended.

2. To serve: spread on small rounds of dark bread with crusts removed.

Makes 4 ounces

ROSE

Roses (*Rosa* species and cultivars) have flavors that are sweet, with subtle undertones ranging from fruit to mint to spice. Almost all roses are edible, with the flavor being more pronounced in the darker varieties. Petals of miniature varieties can garnish ice cream and desserts, or larger petals can be sprinkled on desserts or salads. Freeze them in ice cubes and float them in punches also. Petals are used in syrups, jellies, perfumed butters, and sweet spreads.

Roses can be used to make two kinds of tea, those from the petals and those from the hips. The petals from any fragrant variety that's been grown organically can be used. Rose hips are the cherry-sized red fruits of the rose bush left behind after the bloom has died. Although nearly all rose bushes produce rose hips, the tastiest for eating purposes come from the *Rosa rugosa* or the *Rosa gallica officinalis* variety. The *Rosa rugosa* rose is a variety that's often recommended for both petals and hips because it's a fragrant, pest-free rose that requires no spraying. Rose hip tea is red, with a tart lemon-orange flavor, much like the cranberry, and is a source of vitamin C.

Easy Rose Hip Tea

1 teabag of black tea
1 tablespoon dried rose hips
2 whole cloves
1 cup boiling water
Sugar or honey to taste

1. Place teabag, rose hips, and cloves in a small teapot.

2. Pour boiling water into the teapot.

3. Steep for 5 minutes.

4. Strain and pour into a cup. Sweeten to taste with sugar or honey.

Serves 1

Drying Rose Hips

For those gardeners who are lucky enough to have roses bearing fruit, the fruits can be harvested just after the first frost when they become fully-colored, but not overripe. They should yield to gentle pressure but not be soft or wrinkly. Remove the hairy seeds for they can be a bit irritating to the digestive system. When cooking with rose hips, do not use any metal pans or utensils other than stainless steel or risk discoloration of the fruit and loss of its valued vitamin C stores.

Just after a frost is the best time to gather rose hips. Snap off the tails as you pick them or later when you reach home. Spread the hips out on a clean surface and allow to dry partially. When the skins begin to feel dried and shriveled, split the hips and take out all of the large seeds. After the seeds are removed, allow the hips to dry completely before storing or they will not keep well. Store the dried rose hips in small, sealed plastic bags. These will keep well in the freezer or for several months in the refrigerator.

Rose Water

Rose water is an aromatic, clear, sweet-tasting liquid has been used in perfumery, cosmetics, and medicine for many centuries. In Middle Eastern and West Asian countries, it has long been used as a flavoring in cooking. Rose water is readily available in many international grocery stores. However, if you garden roses, you can prepare rose water at home. The best roses for this are *rugosa* roses. For maximum scent, collect the blossoms as soon as they open, and put them in the water as soon as possible.

The following recipe makes about a quart of excellent-quality rose water in about forty minutes.

2 to 3 quarts fresh roses or rose petals

Water
Ice cubes or crushed ice
1 fireplace brick
Heat-safe stainless steel or glass quart bowl
Large canning pot with a lid
Sterilized quart jar or 2 smaller pint-sized jars

1. Place the brick in the center of the canning pot. Set the small bowl on top of the brick.

2. Place the roses in the pot, adding enough flowers to reach the top of the brick. Pour in just enough water to cover the roses. The water should be just above the top of the brick. Place the lid upside down on the pot.

3. Bring the water to a rolling boil, then lower heat to a slow steady simmer. As soon as the water begins to boil, toss two or three trays of ice cubes or a bag of ice on top of the lid.

4. As the water boils, the steam rises and hits the top of the cold lid, and condenses. As it condenses, water flows to the center of the lid and drops into the bowl. Every twenty minutes, quickly lift the lid and take out a tablespoon or two of the rose water. When there is between a pint and a quart of water that smells and tastes strongly like roses, the rose water is ready and can be bottled. If the roses are simmered in the water too long, the rose essence will become diluted and will smell more like plain distilled water, rather than the heavenly scent of roses.

5. Pour into a sterilized bottle and cap securely, it should need no special preservation other than cool storage.

Makes about 1 quart

ROSEMARY

The small narrow leaves of rosemary (*Rosmarinus officinalis*) have a very spicy odor that makes them valuable as a flavoring and scenting agent. Rosemary has a distinctive pine-woody, camphoraceous scent with a fresh bittersweet flavor. The fresh or dried leaves may be used sparingly for special accent with cream soups made of leafy greens, poultry, stews, and sauces. In olden times, rosemary was believed to stimulate the brain and help the memory and so it came to be associated with remembrance. Before the introduction of refrigeration, rosemary was traditionally used as an antiseptic, astringent, and food preservative. Rosemary can be an effective remedy for digestive upsets and flatulence when taken with food. It stimulates the circulation and rosemary tea can be taken for a nervous headache or used in a compress to be applied to the forehead and temples.

Use a light touch with rosemary, because a little goes a long way! Additionally, pregnant or lactating women should not drink rosemary tea, although they may safely use it in cooking to season food.

Rosemary Tisane

1 teaspoon of dried rosemary leaves or flower tips
1 cup boiling water

1. Place leaves in a small teapot.

2. Pour boiling water over leaves.

3. Steep for 5 to 10 minutes.

4. Strain and pour into a cup. Sweeten to taste.

Serves 1

Lemon-Rosemary Sparkling Tea

8 cups water
12 teabags of black tea
2 tablespoons dried rosemary, crushed
1½ cups sugar
½ cup lemon juice
1 1-liter bottle lemon-lime carbonated beverage, chilled

1. In a large saucepan, bring the water to boiling.

2. Remove from heat. Add tea bags and rosemary.

3. Cover and steep for 15 minutes. Remove and discard tea bags.

4. Add sugar and lemon juice, stirring to dissolve sugar.

5. Strain tea mixture into a large pitcher. Cover and chill in the refrigerator for at least 3 hours or until ready to serve.

6. Just before serving, stir in carbonated beverage.

Serves 12 (8-ounce servings)

SCENTED GERANIUM

Scented geraniums (*Pelargonium* species) come in fragrances from citrus and spice to fruits and flowers, and usually in colors of pinks and pastels. The variety of fragrant foliages and flowers are used in perfume, baking and confections, or in flavoring sauces. The scented geranium has its aroma in its leaves, not its flowers. When the leaves are rubbed, the plants release their perfumes.

Originally from Africa, scented geraniums migrated to Holland and then to England. Over the past few centuries, cultivation has resulted in more than a hundred varieties in an assortment of shapes, flower colors, and perfumes. All are wonderfully fragrant and have a distinctive smell. They combine well with lemon verbena, lemon basil, lemon balm, and mint.

Scented geraniums have a variety of culinary uses, however, not all scented geraniums have tastes that complement cooking. Many cooking recipes use fresh rose-, lemon-, or mint-scented geranium leaves. Basically, their flavors are infused into the dish and then the leaves are removed and discarded before serving. Scenteds are typically used in sweet dishes. Rose varieties add a delicate flavor to sugar which is then used in baked goods or to sweeten teas. Other uses include teas, biscuits, custards, jellies (particularly apple), fruit punches, wine cups, ice cream, and sorbets.

Orange-scented Geranium Iced Tea

2 cups water
4 teabags or 2 tablespoons loose black tea leaves
6 medium fresh orange-scented geranium leaves, washed
8 whole cloves
Thin lemon or orange slices
Crushed ice

1. Warm a teapot.

2. In a tea kettle, bring the 2 cups of water to a boil.

3. Place the tea, geranium leaves and cloves in a warmed teapot.

4. Pour boiling water into the teapot.

5. Cover and steep for 5 minutes. Allow to cool.

6. Fill four tall glasses with crushed ice, pour tea over ice through a strainer, and serve immediately. Sweeten to taste. Garnish with lemon or orange slices, as desired.

Serves 4

Ginger-scented Geranium Honey

4 to 5 tablespoons fresh ginger-scented geranium leaves, chopped
1 pint honey
2 whole cloves
2 allspice berries
Sterilized pint jar

1. In a small saucepan, place geranium leaves in a small saucepan and bruise them with the back of a wooden spoon.

2. Add honey, cloves, and allspice berries. Warm mixture over low heat for a few minutes, stirring well.

3. Pour honey mixture into a sterilized glass jar. Seal tightly and place in a sunny window or warm place for 1 week to 10 days while the flavors blend.

4. Heat honey again until it becomes liquid, then strain out geranium leaves and spices. Pour into a sterilized glass jar and seal tightly.

Make 1 pint

Sweet Violet

Violets (*Viola ordorata*), also known as sweet violets, have a delicate fragrance and leaves. Violets were once used frequently in perfumes, but because its scent quickly dissipates, it has largely been replaced with synthetics in making perfumes.

Many cultures, primarily the Celts and the Germans, celebrated the arrival of springtime at the first sighting of violets. The ancient Greeks combined wine and violets, putting not only the petals in the wine, but also scattered them all about the banquet hall. They also wore garlands decorated with violets in the belief that this would help to prevent dizziness and headaches from overindulging in drink.

Throughout the years people have used violets for medicinal purpose, usually in the form of a tea taken internally. It is reputed to relieve anxiety and insomnia. In the seventeenth century throat lozenges made with violet conserve, were used to treat bronchitis, as well as to combat sinus congestion. Violet sugar was also a popular staple in apothecaries of the time, violets blossoms have antibacterial properties and contain vitamins A and C, and an aspirin-like compound.

In the Victorian times, violets were used in the kitchen and were so popular that they were often served as a confection for high tea. Candied violet petals were used to garnish cakes, pastries, custards, and puddings. Nowadays, the fresh petals are used more often than the candied ones. Violets are also used to add deep color and perfumed taste to jellies, jams, and liqueurs. Parfait Amour, Crème Yvette, and Crème de Violettes are sweet violet liqueurs. Commercially available violet water can be used to add that floral quality to cakes, tea breads, ices, and poached fruit.

Violet Leaf Tisane

2 to 3 teaspoons sweet violet leaves
1 cup boiling water

1. Place leaves in a small teapot.

2. Pour boiling water over leaves.

3. Steep for 5 minutes.

4. Strain and pour into a cup. Sweeten to taste.

Serves 1

Violet Lassi

Lassi is the name given to frothy drinks made with yogurt in place of milk. This is a sour-tart alternative to milk drinks and milk shakes.

1 cup low-fat yogurt
¼ cup fresh or frozen raspberries
2 tablespoons fresh violet flowers and leaves, chopped
2 tablespoons honey
⅓ cup sparkling mineral water

1. In a blender, combine the yogurt, raspberries, violets, and honey.

2. Blend on low speed for 30 seconds, then increase speed to high and blend another 10 seconds, until smooth.

3. Pour violet mixture into 2 glasses and stir in mineral water to taste.

Serves 2

Sweeteners

Flower Sugar

1. Layer fresh or dried flower petals with granulated sugar in an airtight container. Stir daily to keep the sugar from clumping.

2. Once the sugar stays dry and loose, remove the remaining large pieces of the flowers, or grind the entire sugar-flower mixture in a food processor.

Flower Syrup

2 cups water
½ cup fresh or ¼ cup dried flower petals
1 cup sugar

1. In a heavy saucepan, bring water to a boil.

2. Remove from heat and stir in the flower petals. Cover and steep for 30 minutes.

3. Strain and return liquid to the pan. Stir in the sugar. Bring to a boil and cook for 10 minutes.

4. Cool, bottle, and store in the refrigerator.

Makes about 1½ cups

Flower Honey

3 parts honey
1 part fresh or dried flower petals

1. Stir together the honey and dried flower petals, making sure the herbs are totally submerged.

2. Steep in a tightly closed container for one to three weeks, or until the flavor is as desired.

3. Strain to remove the herbs, then store in tightly capped jars.

Lemonades and Spritzers

Jasmine Limeade

2 cups water
1 tablespoon dried jasmine flowers
Chilled prepared limeade
Ice cubes

1. Warm a teapot.

2. In a tea kettle, bring the 2 cups of water to a boil.

3. Place the jasmine flowers in the warmed teapot.

4. Pour boiling water into the teapot.

5. Cover and steep for 5 minutes. Allow to cool.

6. Fill one-half of an 8-ounce glass with the tea poured through a strainer, add ice cubes, and fill with chilled limeade. Stir gently.

Serves 4

Chamomile Pear Cider

2 cups water
1 tablespoon dried chamomile flowers
Chilled pear cider
Ice cubes

1. Warm a teapot.

2. In a tea kettle, bring the 2 cups of water to a boil.

3. Place the chamomile flowers in the warmed teapot.

4. Pour boiling water into the teapot.

5. Cover and steep for 5 minutes. Allow to cool.

6. Fill one-half of an 8-ounce glass with the tea poured through a strainer, add ice cubes, and fill with chilled limeade. Stir gently.

Serves 4

Chamomile Apple Cider

Substitute apple cider for the pear cider in the Chamomile Pear Cider recipe.

Lavender White Wine Spritzer

2 cups water
1 tablespoon dried lavender flowers
Rhine Riesling white wine (sweeter) or California Riesling white wine (dryer)
Chilled club soda
Ice cubes

1. Warm a teapot.

2. In a tea kettle, bring the 2 cups of water to a boil.

3. Place the lavender flowers in the warmed teapot.

4. Pour boiling water into the teapot.

5. Cover and steep for 5 minutes. Allow to cool.

6. Fill one-quarter of an 8-ounce glass with the tea poured through a strainer, one-quarter with wine, add ice cubes, and fill with chilled club soda. Stir gently.

Serves 6

Diabolo Violette Spritzer

2 cups water
½ cup fresh or ¼ cup dried sweet violet flowers
1 cup sugar
Carbonated lemonade

Prepare syrup:

1. In a heavy saucepan, bring water to a boil.

2. Remove from heat and stir in the flower petals. Cover and steep for 30 minutes.

3. Strain and return liquid to the pan. Stir in the sugar. Bring to a boil and cook for 10 minutes.

4. Cool, bottle, and store in the refrigerator.

Prepare spritzer:

1. Fill one-third of an 8-ounce glass with violet syrup, add ice cubes, and fill with carbonated lemonade.

2. Stir gently.

Serves 1

Jasmine Vodka Spritzer

2 cups water
1 tablespoon dried jasmine flowers
½ cup sugar
½ cup fresh lime juice
1½ cups orange vodka
1 cup Grand Marnier
Ice cubes
3 cups chilled club soda
12 lime twists (optional)

1. Warm a teapot.
2. In a tea kettle, bring the 2 cups of water to a boil.
3. Place the jasmine flowers in the warmed teapot.
4. Pour boiling water into the teapot.
5. Cover and steep for 5 minutes. Allow to cool.
6. Strain into a small pitcher, add the sugar and stir well to dissolve the sugar.
7. Stir in the lime juice.
8. Combine the vodka and Grand Marnier with the jasmine syrup.
9. Add the ice and stir briskly until the glass begins to frost, then strain into chilled martini glasses.
10. Top each drink with ¼ cup of the club soda and garnish with a lime twist.

Serves 12

Flower Basket Tea

3 cups water
2½ tablespoons dried sweet violet flowers
2½ tablespoons dried rose petals
2½ tablespoons dried jasmine flowers
1 tablespoon sugar
1 cup of freshly brewed black tea
Ice
Thin orange slice or mint sprig, for garnish

Prepare flower basket syrup:

1. In a heavy saucepan, bring water to a boil.
2. Remove from heat and stir in the violet, rose, and jasmine flowers. Cover and steep for 30 minutes.

3. Strain and return liquid to the pan. Stir in the sugar. Bring to a boil and cook for 10 minutes.

4. Cool, bottle, and store in the refrigerator.

Prepare tea:

1. In a tall glass, combine 1½ tablespoons of the flower basket syrup, 1 tablespoon sugar, and 1 cup of tea. Stir gently and add ice.

2. Serve with a thin orange slice or mint sprig.

Serves 1

Chamomile Iced Tisane Spritzer

2 cups water
4 chamomile herbal tea bags
2 cups ice cubes
1 cup white grape juice
1 cup sparkling water
12 white or red grapes, for garnish

1. Warm a teapot.

2. In a tea kettle, bring the 2 cups of water to a boil.

3. Place the teabags in the warmed teapot.

4. Pour boiling water into the teapot.

5. Cover and steep for 5 minutes. Allow to cool and remove the teabags.

6. Pour the tea into a pitcher; add the ice cubes and the grape juice. Cover and store in the refrigerator until ready to serve.

7. When ready to serve, fill 4 tall glasses with ice. Fill the glasses ¾ full with tea mixture and top them off with sparkling water. Garnish each glass with a few grapes.

Serves 4

Ices and Frozen Treats

Herbal and Floral Ice Cubes

Add an unexpected and delightful touch to ice cubes for your iced drinks. Use flowers and herbs such as rose petals, mint, rose-scented geranium, sweet violets, or lavender.

1. Put one flower, petal, or spring into each ice cube compartment of an ice cube tray.

2. Fill the tray half way full with water and freeze.

3. When frozen, fill the tray completely with water and freeze again.

Strawberry-Rose Petal Ice

2 cups water
½ cup dried rose petals
1 cup sugar
2 teaspoons lemon juice
2 cups strawberry purée (3 cups whole strawberries blended in a blender)
¼ cup low-fat milk

1. In a heavy saucepan, bring water to a boil.

2. Remove from heat and stir in the flower petals. Cover and steep for 30 minutes.

3. Strain and return liquid to the pan. Stir in the sugar and 1 teaspoon lemon juice. Bring to a boil and cook for 10 minutes. Let cool.

4. Combine purée with cooled rose petal syrup, 1 teaspoon lemon juice, and milk.

5. Pour into a loaf cake pan and freeze for 3 hours until firm.

6. Flake with a fork and spoon flakes into chilled serving dishes.

Serves 6 to 8

Easy Lemon-Peppermint Ice

1 cup sugar
½ cup water
¼ cup white vinegar
1 tablespoon lemon juice
3 large sprigs of fresh peppermint
1 12-ounce can frozen lemonade concentrate, thawed
3 cups ice cubes
¾ cup water

1. In a small saucepan, stir sugar and water over medium heat until sugar dissolves. Bring to the boil.

2. Add vinegar and lemon juice and return to a steady boil.

3. Boil over medium heat for 15 minutes until thick, skimming foam off top as required.

4. Add mint sprigs to boiling syrup. Boil for 1 minute, then remove saucepan from heat and let cool

5. Strain syrup. Reserve ½ cup for lemon ice and pour remaining amount into a bottle for storage.

6. In food processor, combine the lemonade concentrate, ¾ cup water, and ½ cup peppermint syrup, and blend all ingredients until smooth.

7. Pour into non-metallic 13 x 9-inch pan and freeze for 45 minutes. Pour mixture back in processor and mix again until smooth. Freeze for 8 hours. Use fork to scrape before serving.

Serves 6

Pineapple-Mint Freeze

1 20-ounce can crushed pineapple
2 tablespoons fresh lemon juice
1 tablespoon fresh coarsely chopped spearmint or peppermint leaves

1. Pour pineapple and lemon juice into an 8 x 8-inch pan and freeze until almost solid.

2. In a blender, combine the frozen pineapple with the mint. Whirl on low speed until smooth but not melted.

3. Serve immediately or return to freezer until serving time. Spoon into parfait glasses.

Serves 4

Raspberry-Hibiscus Sorbet

2½ cups sugar
2 cups water
1 cup dried hibiscus flowers
3 cups raspberry fruit purée (4 cups whole berries blended in a blender)
2 tablespoons lemon juice

1. In a heavy saucepan, bring water to a boil.

2. Remove from heat and stir in the hibiscus flowers. Cover and steep for 30 minutes.

3. Strain and return liquid to the pan. Stir in the sugar, bring to a boil, and cook for 10 minutes. Let cool.

4. Combine purée with cooled hibiscus flower syrup. Pour into a 9- by 12-inch pan until almost frozen.

5. Spoon into a food processor and process until smooth. Return to pan and freeze until solid.

6. Delicious topped with complimentary liqueur or whipped cream.

Serves 6 to 8

Ultimate Hibiscus Slush

1 cup boiling water
1 teaspoon dried hibiscus flower, crushed or 1 red zinger teabag
1 ounce white tequila
1 ounce lime juice
1 ounce Cointreau or orange liqueur
1 teaspoon sugar
10 ice cubes

1. Place hibiscus flower or teabag in a small teapot.

2. Pour boiling water over leaves or teabag.

3. Steep for 5 to 10 minutes.

4. Chill.

5. Strain chilled tea into a blender and add the remaining ingredients and ice cubes.

6. Blend until mixture turns to slush.

Serves 1

Violet Lavender Sorbet

1½ cups water, divided
¾ cup granulated sugar, divided
¼ cup dried lavender flowers
¼ cup dried sweet violet flowers
2 tablespoons lime juice
Cheesecloth
Ice cream maker

1. In a small saucepan, combine 1 cup water and ½ cup sugar. Bring to a boil and continue to cook for 4 minutes. Remove from heat and allow the syrup to cool to room temperature.

2. In a food processor, combine the lavender flowers and ¼ cup sugar. Process for 3 minutes, or until the flowers and sugar are completely blended and in tiny pieces.

3. Add the processed mixture to the cooled syrup and stir well. Allow to stand for 1 hour at room temperature. Strain to remove any particles. Set strained syrup aside.

4. In a nonmetallic saucepan, bring ½ cup water to a boil. Remove from heat and add violets. Allow to steep for 15 minutes, stirring occasionally. Strain through a piece of cheesecloth. Squeeze cheesecloth tightly to release the blue color.

5. Blend the lavender syrup with the violet infusion. Add lime juice. Freeze in an ice cream maker according to manufacturer's instructions.

Serves 4 to 6

Gillyflower Sorbet

1¼ cup water
4 tablespoons sugar
½ cup clove-scented pink (dianthus) flowers
1 tablespoon lemon verbena, finely chopped
Juice of 1 lemon
1 egg white, beaten to frothy peaks
6 whole clove-scented pink flowers for garnish

1. In a small saucepan, combine water and sugar. Bring to a boil and continue to cook for 4 minutes or until sugar is dissolved.

2. Add clove-scented pinks and lemon verbena. Remove from heat and allow the syrup to cool to room temperature.

3. When cool, pour into an ice cube tray without dividers and place in the freezer. After ice crystals have formed, transfer sorbet mixture from tray into mixing bowl, add lemon juice to taste and egg white, and whip. Put back into tray, freeze again, and whip again just prior to serving.

4. Garnish each serving with one perfect clove-scented pink flower.

Serves 6

Violet Milkshake

2 cups water
¼ cup dried sweet violet flowers
1 cup sugar
1 cup low-fat milk
2 to 8 scoops of vanilla ice cream

Prepare violet syrup:

1. In a heavy saucepan, bring water to a boil.

2. Remove from heat and stir in the violet flowers. Cover and steep for 30 minutes.

3. Strain and return liquid to the pan. Stir in the sugar. Bring to a boil and cook for 10 minutes.

4. Cool, bottle, and store in the refrigerator.

Prepare milkshake:

1. In a blender, combine 1½ tablespoons violet syrup, 1 cup of milk, and 2 to 8 scoops of vanilla ice cream.

2. Blend until smooth. Serve immediately.

Serves 1

Sangrias, Party Punches, and Spirits

Lemon Balm Sangria

3 ripe peaches, skinned, pitted, and diced
½ cup lemon balm leaves, chopped
¼ cup lemon verbena leaves, chopped
2 750-milliliter bottles of Gewürztraminer wine

1. In a large pitcher, combine all ingredients and allow to steep overnight in the refrigerator.

2. Strain and serve.

Serves 16 (3-ounce servings)

Lavender Chardonnay Sangria

2 cups water
1 tablespoon lavender flowers
1 lemon
1 orange
½ cup sugar
1 750-milliliter bottle of Chardonnay wine, chilled
1 to 2 cups carbonated water, chilled
2 tablespoons pear cognac
Ice cubes

1. In a tea kettle, bring the water to a boil.

2. Place lavender flowers in a bowl or teapot, and pour the hot water over flowers and let steep for 5 minutes. Strain and let cool.

3. Cut lemon and orange into ¼-inch thick slices. Set aside.

4. Place the 4 end slices from the lemon and orange in a saucepan. Add sugar and ½ cup of the lavender tea to the saucepan to make a fruit syrup. Bring to boiling, stirring till the sugar dissolves.

5. Remove from heat and cool. Squeeze juice from cooked fruit into the syrup. Discard the cooked fruit.

6. In a pitcher, combine the lemon and orange slices, the fruit syrup, wine, carbonated water, and cognac.

7. Serve over ice.

Serves 10 (4-ounce servings)

Mulled Rosemary Tea Wine

1 bottle claret or other full-bodied red wine
4 cups brewed Darjeeling black tea
¼ cup honey
⅓ cup sugar, or to taste
2 oranges, sliced thin and seeded
2 cinnamon sticks
6 whole cloves
3 rosemary sprigs

1. In a medium saucepan, combine the wine, tea, honey, sugar, oranges, spices, and rosemary. Heat over low heat until barely steaming. Stir to make sure honey is dissolved.

2. Remove pan from heat, cover, and let stand for at least 30 minutes.

To serve: heat to just steaming and serve hot.

Makes about two quarts

Rose-scented Geranium Strawberry Punch

Perfect for an afternoon garden party!

3 cups water
6 to 8 rose-scented geranium leaves
1 12-ounce can of frozen pink lemonade
1 10-ounce package of frozen strawberries
1 liter of ginger ale, chilled

1. In a tea kettle or heavy saucepan, bring 3 cups water to a boil.

2. Place rose-scented geranium leaves in a teapot and pour the boiling water the leaves. Cover and let steep for 10 minutes.

3. In a larger pitcher, reconstitute a 12-ounce can of frozen pink lemonade per package directions. Gradually add the herbal tea to the lemonade.

4. Purée a 10-ounce package of frozen strawberries in a blender and add to the lemonade mixture.

5. Add 1 liter of chilled ginger ale.

6. Serve in a large punch bowl.

Serves 24

Fruity Mint Punch

5 cups freshly brewed black tea
2 cups fresh orange juice
¼ cup fresh lemon juice
1½ cups sugar
½ cup water
2¼ tablespoons grated orange rind
½ cup spearmint or peppermint mint leaves, chopped fine

1. In a 2-quart pitcher, combine tea, orange juice, and lemon juice.

2. In a saucepan, combine sugar, water, and orange rind. Heat to boiling over high heat. After boiling for 5 minutes, remove from heat and add mint. Cover and steep for 5 to 10 minutes.

3. Pour fruit syrup through strainer into the pitcher and chill.

4. Serve cold.

Serves 10 (4-ounce servings)

Hibiscus Grape Champagne Punch

2 quarts boiling water
8 teaspoons hibiscus flowers, crumbled
2 24-ounce bottles unsweetened white grape juice
Chilled champagne or ginger ale
Ice cubes
Fresh strawberries

1. In 5-quart, heatproof container or bowl, combine water and hibiscus flowers.

2. Cool tea mixture, stirring occasionally, until it reaches room temperature. Strain.

3. Add grape juice to tea to make punch base. Cover and refrigerate punch base until ready to serve.

4. When ready to serve, place ice cubes in 4- to 6-quart punch bowl and pour punch base over ice.

5. Add strawberries to the punch bowl.

6. Fill punch glasses half full with punch base and fill the remainder with Champagne or ginger ale. Stir.

Serves 24

Lavender Martini

2 cups water
¼ cup dried lavender flowers
1 cup sugar
1½ ounces of vodka or rum

Prepare lavender syrup:

1. In a heavy saucepan, bring water to a boil.

2. Remove from heat and stir in the lavender flowers. Cover and steep for 30 minutes.

3. Strain and return liquid to the pan. Stir in the sugar. Bring to a boil and cook for 10 minutes.

4. Cool, bottle, and store in the refrigerator.

Prepare martini:

1. In a drink shaker, combine 1 tablespoon lavender syrup, 1½ ounces of vodka or rum, and ice.

2. Strain into a chilled martini glass.

Serves 1

Etincelle de Nuit

2 cups water
¼ cup dried rose petals
1 cup sugar
5 ounces chilled champagne

Prepare rose petal syrup:

1. In a heavy saucepan, bring water to a boil.

2. Remove from heat and stir in the rose petals flowers. Cover and steep for 30 minutes.

3. Strain and return liquid to the pan. Stir in the sugar. Bring to a boil and cook for 10 minutes.

4. Cool, bottle, and store in the refrigerator.

Prepare flavored champagne:

1. Place ¾ tablespoon of rose petal syrup into a champagne flute. Fill flute with chilled champagne.

Serves 1

Rose-scented Geranium Raspberry Liqueur

4 half-pints raspberries
1 cup rose-scented geranium leaves
4 cups vodka
½ cup white wine
1 cup sugar
½ cup water

1. In a large jar with a tight-fitting lid, combine the berries, geranium leaves, vodka, and wine. Secure with lid.

2. Place in a cool, dark place to steep for 1 month.

3. After steeping, crush the berries slightly with a wooden spoon or potato masher and steep for another 4 days.

4. Strain the liquid, pressing as much juice as possible from the berries, then strain through a filter.

5. In a small saucepan, combine the sugar and water, and boil until the sugar is dissolved.

6. Cool, then gradually pour and stir into the liqueur, tasting as you go. When the liqueur has reached the desired level of sweetness, bottle and age for an additional 3 weeks in a cool, dark place.

Makes about 1 quart

Rose Cordial

8 cups rose petals
4¼ cups water

½ to 1 pound sugar
4 to 8 cups brandy or vodka
3 sticks cinnamon, broken
½ tablespoon coriander

1. Place 4 cups of rose petals in a large pot and pour 4¼ cups of lukewarm water over the petals. Cover and let stand for 24 hours.

2. Strain the liquid into another pot, squeezing as much liquid out of the petals as possible. Add another 4 cups of rose into the rose water. Cover and let stand for 48 hours.

3. Strain the liquid into another pot, squeezing as much liquid out of the petals as possible.

4. Add the remaining ingredients; use the lesser amount and then adding more to taste. Pour into a jar or container and cap securely with a lid. Let stand for three to four weeks.

5. Strain and bottle.

Makes 1 to 2 quarts

Herbal and Floral Tisane Blends

Tea Party Tisane Blend

1 cup dried rose petals
¼ cup dried hibiscus flowers
½ cup dried lemon balm leaves
2 tablespoons dried orange peel, grated
2 teaspoons whole cloves

Combine all ingredients, blend thoroughly, and store in an airtight container. To make tea, use one heaping teaspoon of blend per cup of water.

Makes 1¾ cups

Lemon Mint Cooler

1 cup dried lemon balm leaves
1 cup dried spearmint leaves
4 tablespoons dried orange peel, grated
½ tablespoon whole cloves

Combine all ingredients, blend thoroughly, and store in an airtight container. To make tea, use one heaping teaspoon of blend per cup of water.

Makes about 2 cups

Soothing Essence Tisane Blend

1 cup dried rosemary leaves
1½ cups dried lavender flowers
1½ cups dried spearmint leaves
½ cup dried chamomile flowers

¼ cup whole cloves

Combine all ingredients, blend thoroughly, and store in an airtight container. To make tea, use one heaping teaspoon of blend per cup of water.

Makes about 4½ cups

Chamomile Rose Herbal Blend

1 cup dried chamomile flowers
1 cup dried rose hips
½ cup dried lemon balm

Combine the dried herbs together, blend thoroughly, and store in an airtight container. To make tea, use one heaping teaspoon of blend per cup of water.

Makes 2½ cups

Pink Rose Tisane Blend

½ cup dried rose petals
2 tablespoons dried lemon balm leaves
½ cup dried clove-scented pink (dianthus) flowers

Combine the dried herbs together, blend thoroughly, and store in an airtight container. To make tea, use one heaping teaspoon of blend per cup of water.

Makes 1 cup

Nitey-Nite Tisane Blend

½ cup dried lemon balm leaves
½ cup dried chamomile flowers

Combine the dried herbs together, blend thoroughly, and store in an airtight container. To make tea, use one heaping teaspoon of blend per cup of water.

Makes 1 cup

Chamomile Apple Tisane Blend

1 cup dried chamomile flowers
¼ cup dried apple bits

Combine the flowers and dried apple bits together, blend thoroughly, and store in an airtight container. To make tea, use one heaping teaspoon of blend per cup of water.

Makes 1¼ cups

Orange Spice Tisane Blend

1 cup dried hibiscus flowers, crumbled
1 cup dried lemon verbena leaves
1 tablespoon dried orange peel, grated
1 teaspoon whole cloves

Combine all ingredients, blend thoroughly, and store in an airtight container. To make tea, use one heaping teaspoon of blend per cup of water.

Makes 2 cups

Flavored Tea Blends

Flavored tea refers to tea leaves flavored with herbs, flowers, and spices.

Southern Mint Tea Blend

¼ cup dried peppermint leaves
1 cup loose black tea leaves
2 teaspoons dried lemon peel, grated
1 teaspoon allspice berries, crushed

Combine all ingredients, blend thoroughly, and store in an airtight container. To make tea, use one heaping teaspoon of blend per cup of water.

Makes 1¼ cups

Night Jasmine Tea Blend

¼ cup dried jasmine flowers
1 cup loose black tea leaves

Combine all ingredients, blend thoroughly, and store in an airtight container. To make tea, use one heaping teaspoon of blend per cup of water.

Makes 1¼ cups

Zingy Tea Blend

¼ cup dried hibiscus flowers, crumbled
1 cup loose black tea leaves
½ stick cinnamon, crushed

Combine all ingredients, blend thoroughly, and store in an airtight container. To make tea, use one heaping teaspoon of blend per cup of water.

Makes 1¼ cups

Apple Spice Tea Blend

½ cup dried applemint or peppermint leaves
¼ cup dried chamomile flowers
1 cup loose black tea leaves
2 teaspoons dried lemon peel, grated
2 tablespoons dried apple bits
½ stick cinnamon, crushed

Combine all ingredients, blend thoroughly, and store in an airtight container. To make tea, use one heaping teaspoon of blend per cup of water.

Makes 1¾ cups

Floral Sachet Tea Blend

1 cup loose black tea leaves
½ cup dried rose petals
2 tablespoons dried jasmine flowers
1 tablespoon dried orange peel, grated
3 stick cinnamon bark, crushed
4 whole star anise, crushed
1 teaspoon ground nutmeg
1 teaspoon whole cloves, crushed

Combine all ingredients, blend thoroughly, and store in an airtight container. To make tea, use one heaping teaspoon of blend per cup of water.

Makes about 1½ cups

Lavender Green Tea Blend

½ cup dried lavender flowers

½ cup dried chamomile flowers
1 cup loose green tea leaves

Combine all ingredients, blend thoroughly, and store in an airtight container. To make tea, use one heaping teaspoon of blend per cup of water.

Makes 2 cups

White-Pink-Rose Geranium Tea Blend

½ cup dried rose-scented geranium leaves, crumbled
½ cup dried clove-scented pink (dianthus) flowers
3 whole cloves, crushed
1 stick cinnamon, crumbled
1 cup loose white tea leaves

Combine all ingredients, blend thoroughly, and store in an airtight container. To make tea, use one heaping teaspoon of blend per cup of water.

Makes 2 cups

Confections

Raspberry and Violet Tarlets

2 cups water
½ cup fresh or ¼ cup dried sweet violet flowers
1 cup sugar
8 ounces puff pastry
1 egg
2 tablespoons corn starch
½ cup milk
½ cup fresh raspberries
4 candied violets, for garnish

Preheat the oven to 350° F.

Prepare violet syrup:

1. In a heavy saucepan, bring water to a boil.
2. Remove from heat and stir in the flower petals. Cover and steep for 30 minutes.
3. Strain and return liquid to the pan. Stir in the sugar. Bring to a boil and cook for 10 minutes.
4. Cool, bottle, and store in the refrigerator.

Prepare tartlets:

1. Roll out the puff pastry dough on a lightly floured surface, and use an upturned bowl to cut out 4 disks of dough, about 6 inches in diameter. Line four 4-inch tartlet molds with the dough, prick all over with a fork, and place into the oven to bake for 12 to 15 minutes, until golden. Let cool.

2. Beat the egg, 5 tablespoons violet syrup, and corn starch in a medium bowl.

3. Heat the milk in a small saucepan. As soon as the milk simmers, whisk it into the egg mixture. Pour back into the saucepan, and return over medium-low heat for 30 to 40 seconds, whisking continuously as the mixture thickens.

4. Pour into the prepared tartlet shells, smooth out the surface with a spatula, and chill for 30 minutes.

5. Cover with raspberries in a circular pattern starting from the center, garnish with candied violets, and serve.

Serves 4

Candied Violets

10 to 12 fresh sweet violets
1 extra-large egg white, at room temperature
Water
Superfine sugar
A small paint brush
Waxed paper

1. In a small bowl, combine the egg white with a few drops of water and whisk lightly until the white just shows a few bubbles.

2. Place the sugar in a shallow dish. If using granulated sugar: put the ½ cup sugar into a blender and whirl until the sugar is broken into smaller crystals.

3. Holding a flower or petal in one hand, dip the paint brush into the egg white with the other hand, and gently paint the flower. Cover the flower or petal completely but not too generously.

4. Holding the flower or petal over the sugar dish, gently sprinkle sugar evenly all over on all sides. Turn the flower so excess sugar falls off, do not shake it.

5. Place the violet on waxed paper to dry. Continue with the rest of the flowers. Let the flowers dry completely by placing the candied flowers in an oven

with a pilot light overnight, or in an oven set at 150° to 200 ° F with the door ajar for a few hours.

6. Store the dried, candied flowers in layers between wax paper in airtight containers until ready to use. They will keep for as long as a year.

Makes about 10

Floral Sprinkles Angel Food Cake

Egg whites from 10 to 12 large eggs
1½ cups sifted powdered sugar
1 cup sifted cake flour or sifted all-purpose flour
1½ teaspoons cream of tartar
1¼ teaspoons orange flower water or orange extract
1 cup granulated sugar
1 cup chopped edible flowers (calendula, clove-scented pink (dianthus), and lavender)
or ½ cup dried edible flower sprinkles
1 cup sifted powdered sugar
2 tablespoons milk or orange juice

Preheat oven to 350° F.

Prepare cake:

1. In an extra-large mixing bowl, allow egg whites to stand at room temperature for 30 minutes. Meanwhile, sift the 1½ cups powdered sugar and flour together 3 times; set aside.

2. Add cream of tartar and 1 teaspoon orange flower water or orange extract to egg whites. Beat with an electric mixer on medium speed until soft peaks form (tips curl). Gradually add granulated sugar, about 2 tablespoons at a time, beating until stiff peaks form (tips stand straight).

3. Sift about one-fourth of the flour mixture over beaten egg whites; fold in gently. Repeat, folding in remaining flour mixture by fourths, along with chopped edible flowers. Pour into an ungreased 10-inch tube pan. Gently

cut through batter with a narrow metal spatula or knife to remove large air pockets.

4. Bake on the lowest rack of the oven for 40 to 45 minutes or until top of cake springs back when lightly touched. Immediately invert cake (leave in pan); cool thoroughly. Using a narrow metal spatula, loosen sides of cake from pan; remove cake.

Prepare icing drizzle:

1. In a large mixing bowl, combine the 1 cup powered sugar, ¼ teaspoon orange flower water or orange extract, and 1 tablespoon milk or juice. Stir in milk or juice 1 teaspoon at a time to make an icing of drizzling consistency.

2. To frost cake, lightly brush off any excess crumbs. Place cake on wire rack over a 15 x 10 x 1-inch baking pan. Use a spoon or ladle to pour icing over cake to cover the cake completely. Let stand 20 minutes. Repeat with a second layer of icing. Let dry 20 minutes. Repeat with a third layer of icing. If necessary, reuse the icing that has dripped on the pan, straining it to remove crumbs. Let icing dry completely. Sprinkle top of cake with chopped edible flowers or snipped dried edible flower sprinkles.

Serves 12

Dried Edible Flower Sprinkles

3 cups fresh calendula, clove-scented pink (dianthus), and lavender flower petals

1. Spread 3 cups edible flower petals in a single layer on two 15 x 10 x 1-inch baking sheets.

2. Let stand 2 to 3 days until completely dry, stirring occasionally to help the drying process.

3. Store remaining sprinkles in an airtight container in a cool, dark place. If using the sprinkles on a confection, then prepare the sprinkles 3 days before you need to use them.

Makes about 3 cups

Candied Rose Hips

Great to snack on!

2 to 3 cups rose hips, freshly picked or purchased
1 cup sugar
½ cup water
1 to 2 pieces of crystallized ginger
Granulated sugar
Waxed paper

1. If freshly picked: Snap off the stems and tail of the rose hips that have been collected. Discard any imperfect ones. Split the hips open. With a teaspoon turned over, force the seeds out of the hips. Scrape out any extraneous membrane from the inside.

2. Place rose hips in a small saucepan, cover with cold water, and bring to the boiling point. Reduce the heat and simmer slowly for 10 minutes. Drain well.

3. In a medium saucepan, combine the ½ cup sugar, water, and ginger. Bring to boiling. Add a cup of the drained rose hip pieces. Cook slowly until the hips just begin to appear translucent.

4. Using a skimmer, remove the hips from the syrup and spread them on a platter to cool. For the second and third cup of hips, cook them in the same way until all are cooked, but never add more than a cupful at a time.

5. When cool, roll the hips in granulated sugar and spread thinly on waxed paper to dry. Store in an airtight, glass container.

Cultivating Culinary Herbs and Edible Flowers

Culinary herbs and edible flowers are relatively easy to grow. The reward of herb and edible flower cultivation is having fresh, flavorful herbs and edible flowers available at your fingertips whenever you want them! Some herbs and edible flowers are annual (calendula, German chamomile, hibiscus), perennial (catnip, mint, dianthus, Roman chamomile, lavender, rosemary), or biennial. Annuals are usually grown from seed; they grow, flower, and produce seed during one season, then die. Perennials stay alive throughout the winter and flower each season. Some herbs are tender perennials and do not survive severe winters and are best grown as annuals or indoors during the winter. Biennials grow for two seasons, flowering the second year only. Some are tolerant to winter temperatures, others are seasonal, or can be grown year-round inside. When buying herbs and edible flowers to plant, check the botanical name to be sure of getting the plant you want.

In addition to furnishing a variety of flavors for use in the kitchen, herbs and edible flowers, because of their ornamental appearance, may be used to good advantage in landscaping to add beauty and fragrance to the home surroundings. They can be conveniently arranged in flower beds, borders, and rock gardens, or assembled in a small formal herb garden convenient to the kitchen, as was the custom in colonial times. If they are grown in rows in the vegetable garden, only a small section will be required to produce enough for family use. The perennials and biennials come up early in spring, and some of them bloom before the annuals are planted. If they are grown on one side or in a corner of the garden or even in flower beds or rock gardens, they will not interfere with the preparation of the garden soil for planting each season. The annuals may be seeded along with other vegetables or they may be arranged in separate beds.

Caution should be used with edible flowers though. Be certain that the flowers are the edible variety, because not all flowers are edible. You may wish to consult a good reference book to find specific edible flowers. Utilize pesticides recommended for fruits and vegetables. Pesticides for use on fruits and vegetables have undergone extensive testing to determine the waiting period between treatment and harvest and potential residuals on food. Pesticides used on flowers and ornamentals have not been evaluated to determine their safety on food crops. Do not eat flowers from florists, nurseries, garden centers, or flowers found on the side of the road, use only flowers that have been cultivated specifically for culinary user by you or someone else.

IN THE GARDEN

In general, one short row or only a few feet of row of each of the annuals or half a dozen plants of the perennials will supply enough herbs and edible flowers for the average family. Herb and edible flower gardens tend to do best when they receive between at least 4 to 6 hours of sunlight per day. The plants can handle a variety of soil conditions, however rosemary requires a well-drained moderately moist soil condition and the mints give the best results on soils that retain considerable moisture but have good drainage. Herbs and edible flowers also tend to thrive in soils that are of low to medium fertility. The soil should be well prepared long enough in advance of planting to allow for settling. If the area has very low fertility, add compost and incorporate it into the soil thoroughly. Since perennials remain in the same location for several seasons, best results may be obtained by adding compost and organic or commercial fertilizers high in phosphorus to the soil before planting. A mulch of straw applied late in fall will prevent winter injury and will aid in starting early spring growth.

INDOORS

A few of the culinary herbs can be grown fairly successfully indoors during the winter, provided favorable growing conditions can be maintained. The annuals mature their fruits or seeds and die at the end of the growing season. They are not so easily grown indoors during the winter as some of the perennials because new plants must be started from seed and this requires considerable care and most favorable growing conditions.

Bring in the herbs and edible flowers that have been growing in containers outdoors all summer or plant seeds and young plants directly into containers using a commercial potting soil mix. For best results, start new plants in the fall by means of rooted cuttings or by crown or root divisions, rather than potting or moving old plants indoors. In order to make sufficient leaf growth for flavoring purposes during the winter, these plants must have plenty of sunlight and a temperature maintained well above freezing at all times. The annuals and biennials that are to be grown indoors in winter should be started from seed sown in outdoor beds sufficiently early in the fall to allow the seedlings to become large enough for transplanting before frost. The perennials can be started as described under propagation, either outdoors early in fall or later in indoor containers.

The most important condition for growing herbs and flowers indoors is bright light. The plants should get 12 to 14 hours of bright light each day. If a windowsill does not provide that much light, alternative lighting can be a fluorescent lighting unit with warm-white and cool-white fluorescent tubes. Temperature is next, with herbs and flowers doing their best at 60° to 70° F during the day and at least 10° cooler at night. Adequate humidity around the herbs and flowers is a third important factor. The air in homes is much drier that in most outdoor environments. Raising the humidity around the plants is as simple as grouping them together or setting them on trays of gravel, sand, or capillary matting.

Water the plants regularly, letting the soil dry slightly between waterings. Fertilize the plants on a regular basis using a water-soluble houseplant fertilizer, in accordance with package directions.

PROPAGATION

The annuals and biennials are grown from seed sown directly in the garden early in spring, while the perennials generally are better started in indoors in containers from seed or cuttings. Most seedlings require temperatures of 60° to 70° F and bright light to grow well. When the plants are about 2 to 3 inches tall and have developed a second pair of leaves, reset them in the garden at the proper time after all danger of frost is gone.

A few plants, such as rosemary, roses, and hibiscus, can be propagated best by stem or root (particularly hibiscus) cuttings. Stems from the latest growth or the upper part of the older stems make the best cuttings and usually can be rooted easily late in summer or early in fall. With a sharp knife, cut the stems into 3-to 4-inch sections, making the cut just above a leaf. Pinch off the lower third of the leaves, taking care not to tear the stem. To prevent wilting, the cuttings should be placed in water or a rooting activator medium as soon as they are removed from the plant.

Cut roots into short lengths 2 to 6 inches long, lay horizontally in a rooting medium and cover with a half-inch of medium. The root cuttings may also be placed upright with the end of the root closest to the stem at the top. Roots that are one-quarter to one-half inch in diameter give the best cuttings.

Plants such as clove-scented pink (dianthus) and lavender can be easily propagated by layering. With layering, rooting occurs while the stem is still attached to the plant. Simply bend a shoot to the ground. Scoop out a small hole where the shoot touches, hold the stem in place, and secure it into place with an old-fashioned clothespin or a hairpin-shaped piece of wire. When the covered parts of the stems have rooted they can be cut from the parent and set as individual plants.

Other plants, such as sweet violets and catnip, can be expanded by division. Divide the crown clumps into individual plants, or clones after one or two seasons' growth. This can be done either in fall or early in spring. These subdivisions can be set directly in permanent locations if made in spring or in containers and brought indoors for winter protection if made in fall.

The mints spread rapidly by means of surface or underground runners that may grow several feet from the parent plant, usually at a depth of 1 to 2 inches beneath the surface. New plants spring up at the nodes of the runners during the season. These plants, with roots attached, can be taken up and transplanted in spring or early in summer, or the runners alone can be planted in rows and covered to a depth of 2 inches.

DISEASES AND INSECT PESTS

Fortunately, the culinary herbs and edible flowers are not especially subject to serious damage by disease or insect pests, particularly when grown on a small scale and may be due somewhat to the repellent or inhibitory action of their aromatic oils. When they are grown on a commercial scale, however, certain diseases and insect pests do cause damage under some conditions. For example, peppermint can be susceptible to several fungus diseases that develop under certain weather conditions. The aphids can be controlled easily with commercial dusts or spray solutions containing nicotine or pyrethrum. The red spider mite and the fungus diseases are more difficult to control, but they present no problem under normal conditions.

However, chemicals for pest control should be avoided, if possible. Pick harmful insects off the plants by hand. Beneficial insects, such as lady beetles and praying mantis, can be used to decrease insect populations. Growing different herbs and flowers together provides diversity to support a good beneficial insect population and keeps pest problems low. Many gardeners place their culinary herbs and edible flower gardens away from other plants to avoid chemical spray drift.

Harvesting and Preserving

The flavor of the different culinary herbs is due for the most part to a volatile or essential oil contained in small glands in the leaves, seeds, and fruits of the plants. The flavor is retained longer if the herbs are harvested at the right time, either for immediate use or preservation for using at a later time. The young tender leaves can be gathered and used fresh at any time during the season, but for winter use they should be harvested when the plants begin to flower and should be preserved promptly. If the leaves are at all dusty or gritty, they should be washed in cold water and thoroughly drained before use or preserving.

The tender-leaf herbs, such as mint, have high moisture content and must be dried rapidly away from the light if they are to retain their green color. If dried too slowly, they will turn dark or mold. For this reason, a well-ventilated darkened room, such as an attic or other dry airy room, furnishes ideal conditions for curing these herbs in a short time. The less succulent leaf herbs, such as rosemary, which contain less moisture, can be partially dried in the sun without affecting their color, but too long exposure should be avoided.

Edible flower flavor can vary with growing conditions and cultivars. Try conducting a taste test before harvesting large amounts of a particular flower. Flowers should be picked in the cool of the day, after the dew has evaporated. Choose flowers at their peak for maximum flavor, avoiding flowers that are not fully open or that are past their prime. To maintain maximum freshness, keep flowers cool after harvest. Long-stem flowers should be placed in a container of water. Short-stemmed flowers should be harvested within 3 to 4 hours of use, placed in a plastic bag, and stored in a refrigerator. Damp paper towels placed in the plastic bag will help maintain high humidity. To keep pollen from distracting from the flavor, remove the pistils and stamens. Additionally, remove the white base of the petal of the flowers, particularly from dianthus and roses, which tends to impart a bitter flavor.

A few plants of the annual varieties should be left undisturbed to flower and mature seed for planting each season. Seeds should be thoroughly dried before storing, to prevent loss of viability for planting and to prevent molding or loss of quality. After curing for several days in an airy room, a day or two in the sun before storing will insure safekeeping.

As soon as the herb leaves or seeds are dry they should be cleaned by separating them from stems and other foreign matter and packed in suitable containers to prevent loss of the essential oils that give to the herbs and edible flowers their delicate flavor. Glass, metal, or cardboard containers that can be closed tightly will preserve the aroma and flavor. Dark glass jars are preferable over clear glass ones, in that they keep light from bleaching the green leaves. If clear glass jars are used to store dried herbs, keep them stored in a dark room to avoid exposure to light.

Drying Herbs and Flowers

The top growth and flowering tops of herbs and flowers, such as mint and lavender, can be tied in small bundles and covered with paper bags and hung in a well-ventilated dark room. Hanging leaves down allows essential oils to flow from stems to leaves. Individual leaves and flowering tops should be spread thinly on screens and dried in the dark (to prevent them from turning dark) as rapidly as possible. The leaves and petals are ready when they feel dry and crumbly in about 1 to 2 weeks.

Some edible flowers dry well, while others lose their flavor during drying. Check by drying a few samples before drying a whole crop. Gather flowers in early morning before the sun shines on them.

After thorough drying, the leaves, flowering tops may be stripped from the stems, and separate flower petals can be packed in containers, such as dark-colored, glass jars with tight fitting lids. Label, date, and store the jars in a dark pantry or cabinet. It is best to use the dried herbs within a year because dried herbs lose much of their flavor or active constituents after a year.

Freezing Herbs and Flowers

Freezing is a particularly effective method for preserving herbs that lose their flavor when dried and for herbs with soft leaves. Mint and sweet violets should be considered to be preserved by freezing in order to maintain their flavor.

Freezing fresh herbs and edible flowers is a relatively simple process. Gently cleanse the herbs or flowers, blot them dry, and remove leaves or petals from the stalks. You can freeze them whole or chopped, packing into bags or airtight containers. A convenient method of freezing chopped herbs or flowers is to simply spoon the clean, chopped herbs or flowers into an ice cube tray, cover each cube with water, and freeze. Then, you can pop them right out of the tray and into a cooking pot or punch bowl as needed. Or, you can puree them in a blender with a small amount of water. Then pour the puree into ice cube trays and freeze. Transfer the frozen herbs or flowers into labeled plastic freezer bags.

Culture Information for Culinary Herbs and Edible Flowers

Calendula (*Calendula officinalis*)

Calendula is an annual, growing 8 to 24 inches tall, depending on the variety. It has oval, pointed leaves on angular stems, with daisy-like flowers in the summer, 2 to 4 inches across in shades of yellow, gold, apricot, or orange.

- Location: Calendula grows best in well-drained soil in full sun, but tolerates partial shade in hot climates.
- In the garden: Space 8 to 12 inches apart or can be grown in containers with good drainage.
- Propagation: Sow seed indoors in early spring or outdoors when all danger of frost is gone. Calendula is self-sowing.
- Care: Grows best in climates with cool summers or in spring and autumn in hotter climates. Remove dead flower heads to prolong flowering. Spray aphids with insecticidal soap. Protect from slugs. Remove mildewed leaves.
- Harvest: Pick leaves when young. Pick flowers as they open, using the petals. Preserve by drying.

Catnip (*Nepeta cataria*)

Catnip is a perennial, growing to 3 feet tall and 2 feet wide. It has sprawling stems with triangular, toothed, 2-inch-long leaves smelling of camphor and thyme. The leaves and stems are covered with downy, white fuzz. Small, tubular, white to pink, edible flowers appear in the summer. The cultivar 'Citriodora' has a lemon scent and flavor.

- Location: Catnip grows best in average, well-drained soil in full sun to partial shade.

- In the garden: Space 12 to 18 inches apart or can be grown in containers with good drainage.

- Propagation: Sow seed directly into the garden in spring or autumn. Catnip is self-sowing. Divide or take cuttings in the spring.

- Care: After the first flowering is finished, cut back several inches to get a second blooming and to maintain shape. Protect from cats.

- Harvest: Pick leaves when young for eating. Pick leaves and flowers when in full bloom for medicinal use or in tisanes. Preserve by drying.

Chamomile, Roman (*Chamaemelum nobile*)
Chamomile, German (*Matricaria recutita*)

Roman chamomile is a perennial, growing to 8 inches tall and 18 inches wide. It has finely cut, feathery leaves, with daisy-like 1-inch flowers in late summer and autumn. German chamomile is an annual that grows to 24 inches tall and 16 inches wide. Its leaves are lightly scented and have a less bitter taste than that of Roman chamomile, and have a slightly higher proportion of the volatile oil that acts as an anti-inflammatory and analgesic.

- Location: Chamomile grows best in sandy, average, well-drained soil in full sun, but tolerates partial shade.

- In the garden: Space Roman chamomile 18 inches apart and German chamomile 6 inches apart. Both types of plant can be grown in containers.

- Propagation: Sow seed directly in the garden in the spring or autumn. Since the cultivars do not produce seed, they must be divided in order to propagate. Divide cultivars in early spring.

- Care: Remove spent flowers.

- Harvest: Pick leaves as needed. Pick flowers the day they open. Preserve by drying.

Hibiscus (*Hibiscus sabdariffa*)

Hibiscus is an annual, bushy, herbaceous shrub growing to 8 feet tall, with smooth or nearly smooth, cylindrical, typically red stems. The leaves are alternate, 3 to 5 inches long, green with reddish veins and long or short petioles. Flowers, borne singly in the leaf axils, are up to 5 inches wide, yellow or buff with a rose or maroon eye, and turn pink as they wither at the end of the day. At this time, the typically red calyx, consisting of 5 large sepals with a collar of 8 to 12 slim, pointed bracts around the base, begins to enlarge, becomes fleshy, crisp but juicy. The capsule turns brown and splits open when mature and dry. The calyx, stems, and leaves are acid and closely resemble the cranberry in flavor.

- Location: Hibiscus grows best in sandy, average, well-drained soil in full sun, but tolerates partial shade.

- In the garden: Space 3½ feet apart or grow in containers with good drainage.

- Propagation: Sow seed directly in the garden. Take root cuttings.

- Care: Should be watered thoroughly and regularly. For best results and lots of blooms, hibiscus should be located where the temperature remains between 60° and 90° F most of the time.

- Harvest: Pick leaves as needed. Pick flowers the day they open. Preserve by drying.

Honeysuckle (*Lonicera japonica*)

Japanese honeysuckle is edible and medicinal. Honeysuckle vines are easy to grow, vigorous, heat-tolerant, and nearly indestructible. The vines are able to climb up to 32 feet high or more, with opposite, simple oval leaves 1 to 2 inches long and sweetly scented double tongued flowers. The flowers are harvested in early morning before they open and are dried for later herb use. The fruit is a dark blue berry 2 to 3 inches diameter containing numerous seeds. The resulting fruit or berries of the honeysuckle flower will provide a fall treat for your local songbirds as well. The berries are very poisonous, do not eat!

The plant is a native of Europe, Eastern Asia, and Japan. However, Japanese honeysuckle is considered an invasive exotic weed in the United States. The problem being that they shade out native plants.

- Location: Honeysuckle grows best in well-drained soil in full sun or some partial shade.

- In the garden: Space 2 to 3 feet apart or grow in containers with good drainage.

- Propagation: Take cuttings in the spring.

- Care: Lightly prune plants until they are well-established at about 2 years old. After flowering, prune for shape.

- Harvest: Pick flowers as they open. Preserve by drying.

Jasmine (*Jasminum sambac*)

Jasmine is an evergreen shrub, with flowers that are ¾-to 1-inch across and are powerfully fragrant, and often reaches 5 feet in height in pots. Jasmine blooms all year long in the greenhouse.

- Location: Jasmine grows best in a well-drained, light soil enriched with leaf mold, peat moss, or compost in full sun to partial shade with intermediate to warm temperatures.

- In the garden: Evergreen shrub growing to 10 feet.

- Propagation: Take cuttings of nearly ripe wood in summer, or ripe wood in autumn or by layers. Transfer cutting to 3-inch pots within 4 weeks, then to 6-inch pots when the 3-inch pots are becoming filled with roots. Jasmines do not like soggy conditions.

- Care: Prune after flowering to keep the plants thinned and shaped. Plants should be pruned regularly to maintain a desired size; some branches may reach 6 to 8 feet long. Pruning also helps keep an abundance of flowers, since flowers are produce on new wood.

- Harvest: Pick flowers as needed. Preserve by drying.

Lavender (*Lavandula angustifolia*)

Lavender is a perennial, growing 18 to 36 inches tall, depending on the cultivar. The plants are bushy to sprawling with small, lance-shaped, greenish-gray leaves, with spikes of lavender flowers in the summer. There are also varieties with purple, pink, and white flowers. French lavender (*L. stoechas*) has large, showy flower bracts.

- Location: Lavender grows best in well-drained soil in full sun.
- In the garden: Space 1 to 3 feet apart or grow in containers with good drainage.
- Propagation: Sow seed indoors. Take cuttings in spring, summer, or early autumn.
- Care: Remove spent flowers. Trim in the spring to maintain size and shape and remove dead wood. Do not prune old wood; it will not regrow.
- Harvest: Pick flowers just as they open. Preserve by drying.

Lemon Balm (*Melissa officinalis*)

Lemon balm is a perennial, growing to 2 feet tall and 2 feet wide. It is a bushy plant with heart-shaped, scalloped-edged, heavily veined leaves. Rubbing the leaves between the fingers releases a minty, lemony fragrance.

- Location: Lemon balm grows best in average, well-drained soil.
- In the garden: Space 2 feet apart or grow in containers with good drainage.
- Propagation: Sow seed indoors. Take cuttings in late spring or early summer. Divide in spring or autumn. Lemon balm also self-sows.
- Care: Cut back after flowering to prevent self-sowing.
- Harvest: Pick leaves as needed. Preserve by drying.

Lemon Verbena (*Aloysia triphylla*)

Lemon verbena is a deciduous shrub, growing to 10 feet tall and 8 feet wide. It has slender branches with lance-shaped leaves and open sprays of white and purple flowers in the early spring.

- Location: Lemon verbena grows best in average, well-drained soil.

- In the garden: Space 3 feet apart or grow in containers with good drainage.

- Propagation: Sow seed indoors. Take tip cuttings in late spring, late summer, or early autumn.

- Care: Prune in the spring to maintain shape and size. Spray spider mites with insecticidal soap.

- Harvest: Pick leaves as needed. Preserve by drying.

Mint (*Mentha* species and cultivars)

Mints are perennials, growing up to 2 feet tall. Oval, pointed, toothed, 2-inch-long leaves in pairs on square stems. Spikes of tiny pink or white flowers appear in summer. Almost all are very easy to grow. Spearmint (*M. spicata*) is considered the best for cooking. Peppermint (*M. piperita*) is rich in menthol and useful in flavoring.

- Location: Mint grows best in average, moist, well-drained soil in partial shade, but tolerates full sun.

- In the garden: Space 2 feet apart or grow in containers with good drainage.

- Propagation: Divide the plants in spring and fall. Take cuttings in the spring or summer. Seldom comes true from seed.

- Care: Grow in large pots, kept either above ground or sunk up to the rim, to restrain invasive roots, or sink barriers, 12 inches into the soil on all sides of the plant. Mint is a very invasive plant. Remove flowers to prevent cross-pollination.

- Harvest: Pick only the top tender leaves for cooking; pick as needed. The flavor is much better when used fresh. Preserve by drying or freezing.

Pink (*Dianthus* species and cultivars)

Pinks are evergreen perennials that form a loose, spreading mat 6 to 12 inches tall. They have long, narrow, blue-to gray-green leaves, with fragrant, edible, single or double, white, pink, red, or bicolored flowers on thin, leafless stems in late spring and summer. There are numerous cultivars of pink, such as the clove-scented pink (*D. caryophyllus*).

- Location: Pinks grow best in well-drained soil in full sun.
- In the garden: Space 1 foot apart or grow in containers with good drainage.
- Propagation: Divide in the summer after flowering. Take cuttings in the spring.
- Care: Remove flower heads to prolong blooming. Spray spider mites with insecticidal soap.
- Harvest: Pick flowers as they open. Preserve by drying.

Rose (*Rosa* species and cultivars)

Rose is a deciduous shrub, growing from less than 2 to more than 20 feet tall. Leaves are composed of pairs of oval, pointed, toothed leaflets on woody, thorned stems, with flowers having five to dozens of petals in pink, red, white, yellow, or orange shades, borne singly or in clusters throughout the growing season. Woody or pulpy rose hips ripen to red, orange, or yellow and are a rich source of vitamin C. The species and older rose varieties have the best herbal properties, such as the white rose (*R. x alba*), gallica rose (*R. gallica*), and damask rose (*R. x damascena*). Some roses with abundant hips are the rugosa rose (*R. rugosa*), eglantine rose (*R. rubiginosa*), and the apple rose (*R. villosa*).

- Location: Roses grow best in humus-rich, moist, well-drained soil in full sun.
- In the garden: Space 3 to 5 feet apart.
- Propagation: Take cuttings in the autumn or grow from seed.
- Care: Prune to shape and remove dead wood in the spring. Spray insect and disease pests with neem.
- Harvest: Pick flowers as they open. Pick hips when they ripen after flowering. Preserve by drying.

Rosemary (*Rosmarinus officinalis*)

Rosemary is a woody, evergreen perennial, growing to 3 feet or more tall and as wide; upright forms can reach 5 to 6 feet tall. Rosemary has gray-green, leathery, resinous, needle-shaped leaves and edible, pale blue, ¼-inch flowers along stems in the spring and early summer. There are cultivars with pink, white, or dark blue flowers and forms with trailing growth.

- Location: Rosemary grows best in average, well-drained soil in full sun.

- In the garden: Space 1 to 3 feet apart or grow in containers with good drainage.

- Propagation: Take cuttings in spring or late summer. Use layering in early summer.

- Care: Trim to shape after flowering. Spray aphids, spider mites, whiteflies, or mealy bugs with insecticidal soap.

- Harvest: Pick leaves as needed. Pick flowers as they open. Preserve by drying or freezing.

Scented Geranium (*Pelargonium* species)

The fragrances of scented geraniums vary from fruity to spicy to even chocolate! Scented geraniums are perennials, growing 1 to 3 feet tall and 1 to 2 feet wide, with velvety leaves, varying from rounded to deeply lobed, plain green to variegated. From summer to autumn, edible five-pedaled flowers appear, varying in color from pink, deep rose, or white. The most widely used scented geraniums for infusion are rose- or lemon-scented.

- Location: Scented geraniums grow best in humus-rich, moist, well-drained soil in full sun to partial shade.

- In the garden: Grow in containers with good drainage.

- Propagation: Take cuttings in the spring, summer, or autumn.

- Care: Trim to shape anytime. Pinch growing tips to promote branching. Spray whiteflies or aphids with insecticidal soap.

- Harvest: Pick leaves as needed. The best fragrance is just before flowers appear. Pick flowers as they open. Preserve by drying.

Sweet Violet (*Viola odorata*)

Sweet violet is a perennial, growing 6 to 12 inches tall. It has heart-shaped, dark green leaves, with five uneven petals in shades of purple, blue, violet, pink, yellow, or white, singly or in combination. The leaves and flowers have medicinal properties and all parts of the sweet violet are edible and it is high in vitamin C.

- Location: Sweet violet grows best in humus-rich, moist soil in partial shade. It often naturalizes.

- In the garden: Space 6 inches apart or grow in containers with good drainage.

- Propagation: Sow seed indoors or outdoors in the spring. It will self-sow and naturalize. Grows best in cool weather.

- Care: Remove faded flowers to prolong flowering. Spray spider mites with insecticidal soap.

- Harvest: Pick leaves in early spring. Pick flowers as they open. Preserve by drying.

About the Author

In her previous books, *Building a Healthy Lifestyle: A Simple Nutrition and Fitness Approach*, *Easy and Healthful Mediterranean Cooking,* and *Flavoring with Culinary Herbs: Tips, Recipes, and Cultivation,* Mary El-Baz presented an invaluable nutritional program for anyone to build a healthy lifestyle, a collection of savory, nutritious Mediterranean recipes, and a guide on using culinary herbs to enhance the flavor, aroma, and appeal of foods making meals pleasant and delightful. She now brings you *The Essence of Herbal and Floral Teas*, a delightful collection of recipes for preparing beverages and sweets using culinary herbs and edible flowers, as well as tips on cultivation for the herbs and edible flowers.

Dr. El-Baz holds a doctorate in Holistic Nutrition from Clayton College of Natural Health and undergraduate and graduate degrees from the University of Missouri.

Index

A

Aloysia triphylla
   See Lemon Verbena 19, 75

C

Calendula 2, 3, 6, 71
   Calendula Herb Tisane Blend 6
   Dried Edible Flower Sprinkles 61, 62
   Floral Sprinkles Angel Food Cake 61
   Orange Spice Calendula Floral Tea Blend 7

Calendula officinalis
   See Calendula 71

Catnip 2, 3, 7, 71, 72
   Catnip Tisane 7
   Peppy Catnip Blend 8
   Smoothing Evening Tisane 8

Chamaemelum nobile
   See Chamomile, Roman 9, 72

Chamomile 2, 3, 9, 34, 35, 38, 54, 55, 72
   Apple Spice Tea Blend 57
   Chamomile Apple Cider 35
   Chamomile Apple Tisane Blend 55
   Chamomile Cooler 9
   Chamomile Iced Tisane Spritzer 38
   Chamomile Pear Cider 34, 35
   Chamomile Rose Herbal Blend 54
   Lavender Green Tea Blend 57
   Nitey-Nite Tisane Blend 54
   Soothing Essence Tisane Blend 53
   Tangy Chamomile Cranberry Tisane 10

Chamomile, German 72
Chamomile, Roman 72

Confections 59
   Candied Rose Hips 63
   Candied Violets 59, 60
   Dried Edible Flower Sprinkles 61, 62
   Floral Sprinkles Angel Food Cake 61

Cultivating culinary herbs and edible flowers 64
   Diseases and insect pests 67
   Drying herbs 69
   Freezing herbs 69
   Harvesting and preserving 68
   In the garden 65, 66
   Indoors 64, 65, 66, 67
   Propagation 66

Culture information for culinary herbs and edible flowers 71

D

Dianthus 3
   Clove-scented Pink Jelly 22
   Dried Edible Flower Sprinkles 61, 62
   Floral Sprinkles Angel Food Cake 61
   Gillyflower Sorbet 44
   Pink Rose Tisane Blend 54
   Tea Sandwich Spread 24
   White-Pink-Rose Geranium Tea Blend 58

Dianthus species and cultivars
   See Dianthus 76
   See Pink 76

F

Flavored tea blends
   Apple Spice Tea Blend 57
   Floral Sachet Tea Blend 57
   Lavender Green Tea Blend 57

Night Jasmine Tea Blend 56
Southern Mint Tea Blend 56
White-Pink-Rose Geranium Tea Blend 58
Zingy Tea Blend 56

H

Harvesting and preserving
   Drying herbs and flowers 69
   Freezing herbs and flowers 69
Herbal and floral tisane blends
   Chamomile Apple Tisane Blend 55
   Chamomile Rose Herbal Blend 54
   Lemon Mint Cooler 53
   Nitey-Nite Tisane Blend 54
   Orange Spice Tisane Blend 55
   Pink Rose Tisane Blend 54
   Soothing Essence Tisane Blend 53
   Tea Party Tisane Blend 53
Herbs and edible flowers 6, 64, 71
   Caribbean Hibiscus Cooler 12
   Catnip Tisane 7
   Chamomile Cooler 9
   Clove-scented Pink Jelly 22
   Drying rose hips 25
   Easy Rose Hip Tea 24
   Fancy Hibiscus Tea 11
   French Garden Iced Tea 16
   Ginger-scented Geranium Honey 29
   Golden Lemon Balm Tisane 18
   Hibiscus Sun Tisane 11
   Honeysuckle Tisane 12
   Hot Jasmine Tea 16
   Jasmine Lemonade 15
   Lavender Rosemary Mint Tisane 17
   Lemon Verbena Syrup 19
   Lemon-Rosemary Sparkling Tea 27
   Orange Spice Calendula Floral Tea Blend 7
   Orange-scented Geranium Iced Tea 28
   Peppermint Tisane 21
   Peppy Catnip Blend 8

Rose water 25
Rosemary Tisane 27
Smoothing Evening Tisane 8
Spring Herbal Tisane 18
Tangy Chamomile Cranberry Tisane 10
Tea Sandwich Spread 24
Violet Lassi 31
Violet Leaf Tisane 30
White Grape and Jasmine Cooler 15
Rose Hip Lemon Tisane 20
Moroccan Mint Tea 21
Rose Hip Lemon Tisane 20
Moroccan Mint Tea 21
Calendula Herb Tisane Blend 6
Hibiscus 2, 11, 49, 73
   Caribbean Hibiscus Cooler 12
   Fancy Hibiscus Tea 11
   Hibiscus Grape Champagne Punch 49
   Hibiscus Sun Tisane 11
   Orange Spice Tisane Blend 55
   Raspberry-Hibiscus Sorbet 42
   Tea Party Tisane Blend 53
   Ultimate Hibiscus Slush 43
   Zingy Tea Blend 56
Hibiscus sabdariffa
   See Hibiscus 73
Honeysuckle 2, 12, 13, 73, 74
   Honeysuckle Tisane 12

I

Ices and frozen treats
   Easy Lemon-Peppermint Ice 41
   Gillyflower Sorbet 44
   Herbal and floral ice cubes 40
   Pineapple-Mint Freeze 42
   Raspberry-Hibiscus Sorbet 42
   Strawberry-Rose Petal Ice 40
   Ultimate Hibiscus Slush 43
   Violet Lavender Sorbet 43

J

Jasmine 2, 14, 15, 34, 36, 74
    Floral Sachet Tea Blend 57
    Flower Basket Tea 37
    Hot Jasmine Tea 16
    Jasmine Lemonade 15
    Jasmine Limeade 34
    Jasmine Vodka Spritzer 36
    Night Jasmine Tea Blend 56
    White Grape and Jasmine Cooler 15

Jasminum sambac
    See Jasmine 14, 74

L

Lavandula angustifolia
    See Lavender 74

Lavender 2, 3, 16, 17, 35, 46, 49, 57, 74, 75
    Dried Edible Flower Sprinkles 61, 62
    Floral Sprinkles Angel Food Cake 61
    French Garden Iced Tea 16
    Lavender Chardonnay Sangria 46
    Lavender Green Tea Blend 57
    Lavender Martini 49
    Lavender Rosemary Mint Tisane 17
    Lavender White Wine Spritzer 35
    Soothing Essence Tisane Blend 53
    Violet Lavender Sorbet 43

Lemon Balm 18, 46, 75
    Chamomile Rose Herbal Blend 54
    Golden Lemon Balm Tisane 18
    Lemon Balm Sangria 46
    Lemon Mint Cooler 53
    Nitey-Nite Tisane Blend 54
    Pink Rose Tisane Blend 54
    Spring Herbal Tisane 18
    Tea Party Tisane Blend 53

Lemon Verbena 19, 75
    Gillyflower Sorbet 44
    Lemon Balm Sangria 46
    Lemon Verbena Syrup 19
    Orange Spice Tisane Blend 55
    Rose Hip Lemon Tisane 20

Lemonades and spritzers
    Chamomile Apple Cider 35
    Chamomile Iced Tisane Spritzer 38
    Chamomile Pear Cider 34, 35
    Diabolo Violette Spritzer 36
    Flower Basket Tea 37
    Jasmine Limeade 34
    Jasmine Vodka Spritzer 36
    Lavender White Wine Spritzer 35
    Violet Milkshake 45

Lonicera japonica
    See Honeysuckle 12, 73

M

Matricaria recutita
    See Chamomile, German 9, 72

Melissa officinalis
    See Lemon Balm 17, 75

Mentha species and cultivars
    See Mint 76

Mint 76
    Apple Spice Tea Blend 57
    Easy Lemon-Peppermint Ice 41
    Fruity Mint Punch 48
    Lavender Rosemary Mint Tisane 17
    Lemon Mint Cooler 53
    Moroccan Mint Tea 21
    Peppermint 3, 20, 21, 76
    Peppermint Tisane 21
    Pineapple-Mint Freeze 42
    Soothing Essence Tisane Blend 53
    Southern Mint Tea Blend 56
    Spearmint 2, 20, 76
    Spring Herbal Tisane 18

N

Nepeta cataria
    See Catnip 7, 71

P

Pelargonium species
    See Scented Geranium 28, 78
Pink 3, 22, 76, 77
    Clove-scented Pink Jelly 22
    Floral Sprinkles Angel Food Cake 61
    Gillyflower Sorbet 44
    Pink Rose Tisane Blend 54
    Tea Sandwich Spread 24
    White-Pink-Rose Geranium Tea Blend 58

R

Rosa species and cultivars
    See Rose 24, 77
Rose 3, 20, 24, 25, 28, 47, 51, 77
    Candied Rose Hips 63
    Chamomile Rose Herbal Blend 54
    Drying rose hips 25
    Easy Rose Hip Tea 24
    Etincelle de Nuit 50
    Floral Sachet Tea Blend 57
    Flower Basket Tea 37
    Pink Rose Tisane Blend 54
    Rose Cordial 51
    Rose water 25
    Spring Herbal Tisane 18
    Strawberry-Rose Petal Ice 40
    Tea Party Tisane Blend 53
Rosemary 3, 26, 27, 69, 77, 78
    Lavender Rosemary Mint Tisane 17
    Lemon-Rosemary Sparkling Tea 27
    Mulled Rosemary Tea Wine 47
    Rosemary Tisane 27
    Soothing Essence Tisane Blend 53
Rosmarinus officinalis
    See Rosemary 77

S

Sangrias, Party Punches, and Spirits 46
    Etincelle de Nuit 50
    Fruity Mint Punch 48
    Hibiscus Grape Champagne Punch 49
    Lavender Chardonnay Sangria 46
    Lavender Martini 49
    Lemon Balm Sangria 46
    Mulled Rosemary Tea Wine 47
    Rose Cordial 51
    Rose-scented Geranium Raspberry Liqueur 51
    Rose-scented Geranium Strawberry Punch 47
Scented Geranium 78
    Ginger-scented Geranium Honey 29
    Orange-scented Geranium Iced Tea 28
    Rose-scented Geranium Raspberry Liqueur 51
    Rose-scented Geranium Strawberry Punch 47
    Spring Herbal Tisane 18
    White-Pink-Rose Geranium Tea Blend 58
Sweet Violet
    Candied Violets 59, 60
    Diabolo Violette Spritzer 36
    Flower Basket Tea 37
    Violet Lassi 31
    Violet Lavender Sorbet 43
    Violet Leaf Tisane 30
    Violet Milkshake 45
Sweeteners 32
    Flower Honey 32
    Flower Sugar 32
    Flower Syrup 32

V

Viola odorata
    See Sweet Violet 79

978-0-595-41026-2
0-595-41026-X